UNDERDOG MARKETING

UNDERDOG MARKETING

Successful Strategies for Outmarketing the Leader

Edmund Lawler

 **MASTERMEDIA LIMITED**
NEW YORK

MASTERMEDIA and colophon are registered trademarks
of MasterMedia Limited.

    p.   cm.
ISBN 1-57101-053-X : $19.95

95-079363
CIP

Designed by Virginia Koenke Hunt
Manufactured in the United States of America

DEDICATION

In loving memory of my brother Dan

(1963–1982)

TABLE OF CONTENTS

4 The Reinventors

These five concerns radically changed the nature of their
markets, often bypassing established competitors. They are:
1-800 Flowers, Nor'Wester Brewery and Public House,
Houston's Second Baptist Church, Viking Office Supply and
Christian Supply Centers.

5 The Perfecters

These four companies use a larger rival's basic gameplan but
articulate it to perfection and gain share in the market.
They are: Computer City, Gateway 2000, Meridian Bancorp
and Allen-Edmonds Shoes.

6 The Shadow Casters

These four companies cast a larger shadow on the market
than their actual selves by building credibility in the critical
early years of a company. They are: Devon Direct Marketing
and Advertising, Thrifty Rent-A-Car, Stratco and Sweet Talk
Productions.

7 Conclusion: Tactical Advice for Underdog Marketers

Twenty practical, tactical tips to outmarket the leader.

1 Introduction:

The Strategies and Principles of Underdog Marketing

Everyone loves the underdogs, those feisty challengers to the market leaders. Unlike market leaders, which are often hamstrung by tradition and unwieldy bureaucracies, underdogs are close to the ground and quick to market. They love the thrill of risk and innovation.

It's no wonder that an industry's most innovative practices are often the creation of the No. 2 player. It's the natural scrappiness and ingenuity of underdogs that make them so fun to watch in their quest to outmarket the leader.

Although public opinion usually places the underdog on the side of the angels, a subordinate position in the market is fraught with danger. An underdog's marketing practices don't have to be as good as the leader's, they have to be better. An underdog content with the status quo is not long for this world. Big dogs have a way of snapping back when their cages get rattled.

In the decade's most dramatic marketing dogfight, AT&T, the

No. 1 long-distance carrier, has ferociously resisted MCI's challenge with price cuts and hard-hitting advertising. A war of words by both parties has been called "trash talk" by some.

Ever the provocateur, MCI, according to MCI's president, Timothy Price, says it's delighted that AT&T stepped down from its pedestal to "knife-fight with us in the gutter."

Not every underdog is as eager to antagonize the leader as is MCI. In fact, most underdogs in this book have found ways to make a profit or gain market share, or both, without directly challenging the leader.

John Stollenwerk, president of Allen-Edmonds Shoe Corporation, a $55 million maker of men's dress and casual shoes, says his company prefers not to rile the shoe industry's big players. "It would be stupid on our part. It's like kicking an elephant to see if it will move. Obviously, the elephant can return the kick with a lot more force." Allen-Edmonds has quietly carved out a niche for itself by perfecting the comfort and fit of its meticulously handcrafted shoes, which command a premium price.

Regardless of how quietly a smaller competitor may be operating, if it consistently does things better than the market leader, the underdog had better beware, warns David Tait, executive vice president of Virgin Atlantic Airways. "If you're doing what you're doing very well, there's no way it won't attract the attention of the industry giant. You don't even have to be stealing huge amounts of business from them because they'll notice. And when they do, you'd better be ready."

Underdog Marketing profiles 25 companies to help get "you" ready. Their marketing stories are told in the words of their founders, CEO's, marketing directors or other top executives. They are street-level pragmatists, not marketing theoreticians.

The companies represent a wide variety of enterprises— from a microbrewery in Oregon to a Baptist church in Texas. The book includes a British-based airline and a Canadian hardware retailer.

From the United States, there are financial services companies, consumer goods marketers, bookstores, consulting firms, services providers and a computer maker.

Many marketing battles are fought on the advertising front. *Underdog Marketing* goes beneath the veneer of advertising to explore how companies orchestrate their entire marketing mix to challenge a leader or group of leading companies. Several companies in this book don't advertise at all, preferring to use other promotional techniques. Pricing, distribution and product development strategies are explored.

Although each story is unique, a number of universal underdog marketing principles are identified in this introductory chapter. The 25 companies have been broken into five chapters based on the company's dominant outmarketing strategy. Some final lessons on outmarketing the leader are presented in the last chapter.

There are five breeds of underdog marketers:

■ **The Challengers.** The most aggressive underdog marketers, these companies get right in the face of their larger rivals. They name names in their advertising and don't hesitate to bad mouth the big dogs. Some cut prices; others charge a premium. Some innovate, while others prefer to emulate and let the leaders bear the high research-and-development costs.

■ **The Differentiators.** These underdog marketers don't usually fly in the face of their larger rivals but prefer to markedly distinguish their product or service from a larger competitor or group of competitors.

■ **The Reinventers.** By radically changing the nature of their industry, these underdog marketers often bypass larger, more established competitors.

■ **The Perfecters.** These underdogs use a larger rival's game plan, but articulate it to perfection and gain share in the market.

■ **The Shadow Casters.** Proving that mind share is as important as market share, these underdog marketers cast a larger-than-life shadow in the market, to build credibility and momentum in the critical early years of a company.

Here are ten principles that underdog marketers use to outmarket the leader. Examples, drawn from the 25 company profiles, follow each principle.

1. **Underdogs motivate employees by emphasizing the greater size and might of a competitor and by reminding employees that it's not the size of the dog in the fight but the size of the fight in the dog. Some underdogs go so far as to demonize the leader.**

   Firing up the troops to tackle the industry's titan puts the underdog on the side of angels, notes MCI's Timothy Price. "It's easier to convince your employees that what we're doing is more than just a business. It's a crusade against a much larger company that we believe has tried to deny Americans the right to choose their own long-distance service."

2. **Unless they're the low-cost producer, underdogs rarely challenge a leader to a price war. Big dogs have deep pockets and can generally win a war of attrition.**

   "Don't pick fights you can't win," says John Katzman, founder and president of test-preparation company The Princeton Review. "There are certain places where large companies have an advantage." That includes price. "The bigger companies can keep their prices down until you are gone."

3. **When directly challenging a leader, underdogs use 'corporate judo' to force the big dog to turn its weight and size upon itself.**

   Disposable diaper maker Drypers found a way to redirect the aggressive couponing and momentum of its large rival Procter & Gamble by issuing 'convertor' coupons. Shoppers who presented one of P&G's Pampers coupons along with a Drypers' convertor received $2 off on a bag of Drypers. Retailers unwittingly aided Drypers by sending the Pampers coupons to P&G instead of Drypers for redemption.

4. **Underdogs bark like the big dogs by taking on the look and feel of a leader. They cast a larger-than-life shadow on the market to establish credibility and momentum.**

Thrifty Rental Car took on all the trappings of a Hertz and Avis, even though it was substantially smaller. "We decided to look just like the big guys," says Thrifty's Meloyde Blancett-Scott. Thrifty created signage, attractive-looking counters in its rental centers and well-crafted advertising to elevate itself to the same field as the leading players.

5. **Underdogs create a distinctive personality. Youthful, hip, irreverent—even brash personalities are more engaging and more memorable.**

Virgin Atlantic Airways flies under one of the most unique labels in the air. "The Virgin name is gaining awareness all over the world. It's a wonderful name because it's different and innovative," says Virgin's David Tait. Virgin backs up its unique name with a raft of quirky service amenities that contribute to its mystique. The brand name has proved a valuable weapon in its noisy dogfight with British Airways.

6. **Rather than challenge a leader head-on, underdogs differentiate their product or service from the leader's. Unless it poses a direct competitive threat, the leader won't pursue an underdog into a niche.**

Edward D. Jones has opened more offices than any brokerage on Wall Street. Yet, industry leaders Merrill Lynch and Paine Webber have paid scant attention to the underdog. Why? Because St. Louis-based Jones pursues a different breed of customer.

Jones caters to older, conservative "buy-and-hold" investors found in smaller towns across America. There's no room for risk in their portfolios. Wall Street is not their style, which explains why Jones has an office just about everywhere but Wall Street.

7. **An underdog stakes its reputation on such characteristics as innovation, remarkable customer service, best price or highest-quality product. It then communicates to its customers whichever is the strongest of these attributes.**

   1-800-FLOWERS is best known for its reinvention of the floral industry through its freshness guarantees and leading-edge order and delivery practices; the Tattered Cover bookstore, for its painstaking attention to customer service; and Allen-Edmonds, for the fine craftsmanship of its shoes. Each company plays to its strongest suit in its customer communications and does not attempt to overwhelm readers or viewers with too many attributes.

8. **If a dogfight erupts, the underdog responds swiftly and loudly. The media and the public love a good fight and will often empathize with the underdog.**

   Virgin Atlantic responded quickly to a British Airways ad whose headline stated: "More people choose British Airways to London than any other airline." Copy ended with the word "Duh" as if to suggest that British Airways' claim of superiority was a no-brainer.

   Several days later, Virgin bit back with a two-page spread in the *New York Times.* On one page was a reprint of the British Air ad. The headline on the opposite page stated: "More people switch to Virgin Atlantic from British Airways than from any other airline. Ha!"

   The media quickly seized on this skirmish in the airlines' long-running feud.

9. **Barring a price war, the market leader's prices can serve as a base from which a service-savvy or quality-conscious underdog can charge a premium.**

   Children's Discovery Center, confident that its curriculum and services were superior to rival KinderCare's, charges parents a premium over the price of the large child care chain. The Princeton Review (TPR) regards its larger rival's price structure as an industry standard, which supports its own premium price. TPR rationalizes its higher price on the strength of its classes and superior customer service.

10. **Smart use of technology by an underdog can level the playing field. The trick is to get wired first or become better wired than the top dog whose breadth is often a disadvantage.**

    As the smallest of the big banks in Pennsylvania, Meridian Bancorp got an edge on the big dogs by harnessing the best and the brightest that technology can offer. Meridian's new tools allow it to better identify its best customers, as well as serve them more efficiently.

2 The Challengers

Imagine taking on the likes of AT&T, Procter & Gamble or British Airways. Between them, they generate more than $110 billion in revenues. All three are world-class marketers, but that's hardly stopped three underdog marketers from undertaking the exhilarating challenge of outmarketing the leader.

MCI, Drypers and Virgin Atlantic Airways challenge the leaders in their respective markets head-on. It's risky business, but no market leader is invincible.

While the underdogs' pricing, promotion, distribution or product strategies to challenge the leader are often vastly different, all three companies practice a form of corporate jujitsu. The idea is to force the market leader to turn its size and its might on itself.

A fourth Challenger profiled in this chapter, The Princeton Review (TPR), has Kaplan Educational Centers, a standardized test-prep industry leader, on the run with a mix of innovations, customer service initiatives and even a few mocking ads. TPR's fiery founder, John Katzman, warns underdog marketers: "Don't pick fights you can't win. There are certain places where large companies have an advantage."

The fifth Challenger is Muriel Siebert & Co., a discount brokerage firm founded by the first woman to hold a seat on the New York Stock Exchange. In addition to the challenge of proving that women belong on Wall Street, Muriel Siebert has had to wrestle away customers from the big discount securities firms such as Charles Schwab, Quick & Reilly, and Fidelity Brokerage Services. Her best advice: Never promise more than you can deliver.

This chapter examines how these five challengers have cleverly thrown the big dogs off balance to seize, and then keep, some of their customers.

In the decade's most high-profile marketing battle, MCI has used lower prices, innovative new products and a fresh, almost sassy, personality to attract new customers. Its "Friends and Family" discount calling program has been hailed as one of the most brilliant marketing initiatives ever.

Drypers has lured Procter & Gamble into a brutal disposable diapers price war. Thanks to its low overhead and flexible workforce, Drypers is not only surviving, but steadily gaining in its efforts to keep the bottoms of America's babies dry.

Despite the innocence of its name, Virgin Atlantic plays tough with its large arch rival by directly targeting British Airways passengers with offers of free travel on Virgin. The airline delights in making British Airways look bad by pampering its "upper class" passengers with a raft of tough-to-match amenities.

Virgin didn't necessarily set out to antagonize British Airways, but David Tait, Virgin's executive vice president, says, "Be prepared to pay the price for doing things right, because the leader will eventually come knocking."

Now, meet the Challengers.

MCI

Challenging AT&T, whose reliability, familiarity and trustworthiness earned it the moniker "Ma Bell," seems as sacrilegious as burning the American flag. Its sterling reputation notwithstanding, AT&T was ripe for competition in the dynamic new world of deregulated long-distance phone service.

MCI, a feisty underdog, put a sizable chink in AT&T's once impregnable armor through a series of bold marketing strokes that clearly caught the telecommunications industry's top dog off guard.

MCI's innovative "Friends and Family," a discount long-distance calling program, helped bring millions of new customers into its fold at the expense of AT&T.

For those keeping score, MCI runs giant, outdoor, digital tally boards in a dozen cities that calculate in real-time to the penny how much MCI customers have saved by jumping AT&T's ship.

By getting family members and friends to call one another and describe the benefits of joining a calling circle, MCI simultaneously boosted its brand awareness and put the feet of millions of instant sales reps on the street. It was network marketing taken to new heights.

Posing a Serious Threat

AT&T no longer takes lightly the threat posed by MCI, whose long-distance market share grew steadily from 13 percent in 1990 to about 20 percent in 1995, though the company is only one-fifth the size of AT&T.

Ma Bell's ferocious counter-offensives and MCI's equally vitriolic responses over the airwaves and in the press have become the stuff of one of the most expensive, high-profile marketing battles ever waged. It makes the storied clashes between Pepsi and Coke or Avis and Hertz seem almost like child's play.

In 1993 alone, AT&T spent $461 million and MCI $199 million on media advertising to trumpet its long-distance services. That's

$660 million to influence consumers and businesses on what some would say is one of life's truly mundane decisions—choosing a long-distance service.

Jockeying for Pole Position

It's serious business to MCI and AT&T. At stake is control of the burgeoning $70 billion long-distance market. Longer-term, AT&T, MCI and smaller rivals like Sprint and LDDS are jockeying to best position themselves as the predominant supplier of telecommunications services on the information superhighway.

Long-distance telephone service is just a foot-in-the-door tactic for the telecoms who in the next decade are eager to offer more data, wireless and teleconferencing services. The company with the most familiar, likable brand is likely to be the player who serves up the lion's share of the hot new services of the 21st century.

In the Hot Seat

Timothy F. Price, MCI's president and COO of MCI Telecommunications, Inc., has been on the firing line in the no-holds-barred battle for market share against AT&T. As the head of MCI's Atlanta-based business markets division in the early 1990's, Price directed efforts to outmarket AT&T. He was credited with generating some of the company's most clever, ambitious marketing plans, which gained MCI one million of AT&T's former customers.

By the end of 1994, when AT&T had recouped those one million customers through its "True USA" discount calling program, Price was summoned to MCI's Washington, D.C., headquarters to help regain MCI's former momentum. With overall responsibility for both the business and consumer markets, Price is applying several key maneuvers from his Underdog Marketer's playbook to keep the heat on AT&T. They include:

■ **Practicing corporate jujitsu.** In short, this strategy calls for the challenger to force the market share leader to use its own weight and size against it. By re-writing the rules of the marketplace, the larger rival is thrown off balance.

"The best way to do that is through speed of execution," says Price. "The smaller company can react and bring things to market before the larger player can."

When AT&T reacts with a discounting program, it must discount a much larger volume of calls than MCI. "Because AT&T controls about 70 percent of the consumer market, it must discount seven of every 10 calls made. But in our case, it's only two of 10 because of our 20 percent market share. It's more expensive for the market share leader to react." MCI proves that might doesn't make right.

■ **Motivating employees.** Firing up the troops to tackle the industry's titan puts the underdog on the side of angels, notes Price.

"What helps us is that we have an enemy to focus on. And the enemy, God bless them, is so vicious, so big, and so formidable that the meaner their advertising gets and the more mean-spirited their public comment gets, the more enthusiastic our people become.

"When Joe Nacchio (president of AT&T's consumer division) is quoted in *USA Today* as saying that MCI can't compete with AT&T, we put that quote on every bulletin board in every one of our customer service centers and sales centers in the country. It's an incredible motivator."

By demonizing the larger competitor, MCI builds a fire in the belly of its relatively young work force. MCI captured that firebrand spirit in a series of television spots starring its own well-scrubbed employees in a warehouse-sized call center where they were seen furiously enlisting new customers.

Not only are MCI employees instilled with an almost messianic zeal to sell its services to AT&T customers, but also to sell to their own friends and family. "It wasn't just our telemarketers and our sales people, it was our lawyers, our construction workers, our human resources employees. They all became missionaries for 'Friends and Family.' "

MCI equipped its employees with little cheat sheets from which they could recite five key features and benefits of "Friends and Family" to people they met at picnics or cocktail parties. Employees eagerly preached the gospel of MCI.

■ **Strike quickly with innovations.** By virtue of its size and its entrepreneurial nature and structure, the time between the spark of a new idea and the actual introduction of a new MCI service can be as little as 70 days.

For example, MCI developed and launched 1-800-COLLECT, a discount collect-call service, in only 70 days. The program allows callers to access MCI's network directly, bypassing AT&T or the new breed of phone company entrepreneurs whose rates border on piracy.

MCI exploited the fast-growing market before AT&T even had the chance to consider the wealth of opportunities the market holds. AT&T fired back with the clumsily titled 1-800-OPERATOR. But by that point, MCI had already staked out some lucrative and previously overlooked turf.

Foregoing its brand name, MCI chose to make 1-800-COLLECT a brand unto itself, a strategy Price likens to Saturn establishing its unique brand within General Motors.

Other lightning-quick MCI rollouts include Proof Positive and networkMCI BUSINESS. To counter AT&T's claims that it offered the lowest possible rates to small and medium-sized businesses, MCI quickly crafted the Proof Positive system that guaranteed its business audience rates that were more favorable than AT&T's. A business customer's account is reviewed every quarter. Time to market: 90 days. NetworkMCI BUSINESS, a plan that uses a variety of high-tech telecommunications tools to help a business solve its problems, was signed, sealed and delivered to the market in only 110 days.

In May, 1995, MCI took a bold step when it announced a $2 billion investment in media giant and fellow marketing maverick News Corporation. The alliance will be critical to the success of both companies in the 21st century, as will MCI's earlier alliance with British Telecommunications PLC, which owns a 20% stake of the company.

■ **Allow no safe harbors.** Despite being only a fifth the size of its $70 billion rival, MCI will never concede a market segment to AT&T. When the government ruled that 800 numbers could become "portable," MCI aggressively invaded that harbor.

Once again, MCI turned to its employees who were asked to carry a pad with them everywhere they went in an effort to record any 800 number they saw. They found numbers on the sides of buses and on the inside panels of refrigerators.

MCI fired up its employees by telling them that AT&T had been "the warden of the 800-number prison" for 25 years and that customers were at last free to scramble over the wall to seek out a carrier of their choice. The program, dubbed "Project 800" succeeded because MCI leveraged the zeal of its employees.

Armed with those numbers, MCI could then call the companies and invite them to move their 800 service from AT&T to MCI. "The campaign was similar to 1-800-COLLECT. Because AT&T owned those markets for so long and didn't have effective competition, they could command any price they wanted. That's why we have to be everywhere," says Price.

To allow AT&T to operate in a safe harbor is to allow them to operate at high margins. The revenues generated by AT&T in the safe, non-competitive harbors can then be used against MCI in more competitive arenas.

"We try to be everywhere," says Price, "but being smaller than AT&T we can't market as intensively in every harbor. We apply a major thrust in one area and then move quickly to another. We try to do what (the late University of Alabama football coach) Paul 'Bear' Bryant told his team: 'Be mobile, agile and hostile. That way your opponent never knows where the next punch is coming from.'"

MCI's Chairman and CEO, Bert Roberts, upon being named *Advertising Age*'s "Adman of the Year," said, "As long as we can keep

AT&T wondering what we are going to do next and trying to copy it, it leaves us free to concentrate on people and what they want from long-distance service. That, quite simply, is our secret."

Roberts, an amateur magician, is fond of pulling coins out of unexpected places.

■ **Create a distinctive personality.** MCI has artfully portrayed itself as the fresh-faced, sometimes irreverent upstart: The Underdog. That gritty, youthful persona is conveyed in many of MCI's marketing messages.

There's nothing coincidental about the youthful look to MCI's marketing messages. The company's target market is the college-aged population through the Baby Boomers—mobile populations who rely on long-distance phone service to stay in touch with friends and family scattered across the globe.

In a series of spots created by the Messner Vetere Berger McNamee Schmetterer agency, MCI seems oblivious to the long shadow cast upon the market by AT&T. The nearly 200 commercials brand MCI as the leading-edge carrier favored by bright, friendly-looking folks who enjoy MCI's low prices as they keep in touch with old college roommates or parents in another corner of the country.

"We clearly want to be perceived as hip, fun, current and a part of pop culture. And we want to be known as the company that brings people closer to the people they love most," says Price.

Not all of MCI's ads are quite so chipper, however. About a fifth of the company's 250 television spots rolled out in the course of a year take direct aim on AT&T. In one, a twenty-something MCI telemarketer coyly states that she hopes she's not making AT&T nervous as she contacts their customers to alert them to the potential savings by switching to MCI.

In another spot, as well as in print ads, MCI sounds more strident, almost desperate as it states "Shame on You AT&T." The ad was in response to claims made by AT&T in its successful "True USA" counter-offensive.

In yet another long-running series of spots, MCI uses an imitation Jeopardy board and the voice of Dan Pardo to ridicule AT&T's claims of better service or price.

"I want the True-False to become ingrained in the culture," says Price. "When someone makes a false claim like AT&T [has], I want people to hear that 'BUZZ' in their head and recall the jingle: 'It just doesn't ring true.'"

This leads to another important tactic from the MCI playbook:

■ **Respond swiftly and certainly to a larger competitor's claims and charges or other forms of retaliation.** Despite AT&T's formidable marketing firepower, which Price estimates is four times what MCI can muster, no volley goes unanswered.

"It's important to quickly rebut a larger competitor's false claims because they have budgets to say it longer and louder than a smaller company. If a lie gets repeated a thousand times, it can assume the ring of truth. We are always ready for their response."

MCI sets the record straight for another critical reason, explains Price. At the corporate level, a decision-maker who specified MCI long-distance service over AT&T may get an uneasy feeling when his or her boss encounters an AT&T claim in print or broadcast that undermines MCI.

Likewise, a consumer who recommends a friend or family member join his or her MCI calling circle feels sheepish if AT&T's marketing paints "Friends and Family" as a bad deal.

"Our customers are emotionally connected to us," says Price. "When AT&T criticizes us, our customers get very riled up about it. If we don't respond vigorously in their face, our customers call us and say: 'Why aren't you answering them?' Our customers have made an investment in MCI and they feel like they are being personally attacked."

MCI Raises its Profile

Co-founded in 1968 by the late William McGowan, MCI initially provided telecommunications services only to businesses. Today, the business segment makes up only 55 percent of total; the balance of the company's $14 billion in revenues comes from the consumer side.

MCI launched its first television campaign in 1984 based on the claim its rates were lower than AT&T's. By that point, MCI had begun spreading its wings and was offering its services to consumers, as well.

In 1990, MCI formed a Consumer Markets Division and tripled the amount it was spending on advertising. AT&T, which had largely ignored MCI's growing presence in the 1980's, began to take notice. Lawsuits over unfair advertising were exchanged. The gloves were off and the American public was about to get ringside seats at one of the classic battles in American marketing.

Some dismissed the mudslinging as childish, but there was nowhere to hide. MCI's efforts to outmarket AT&T have saturated the airwaves ever since.

"At first, AT&T didn't even want to recognize our existence," says Price. "That's the classic strategy of market leaders. The big guy doesn't recognize the little guy for fear of granting them additional credibility. AT&T had done that for years."

AT&T Bites Back

But as MCI grew more apparent on AT&T's radar screen, the top dog bit back by launching its "Put it in writing campaign," in which AT&T encouraged its customers to demand that competitors put their savings claims in black and white.

"The whole idea was to slow down MCI's marketing momentum. Our telemarketing machine was taking 100,000 AT&T customers every week," says Price. "If you're the market leader, you want to paralyze the market and maintain the status quo. Inertia works to your advantage. Until the 1984 divestiture, AT&T held 100% of the market, then 90, 80 and today less than 70 percent. It behooved AT&T to inject fear, uncertainty and doubt everywhere. That was their strategy that began to emerge about 1990."

AT&T's "Put it in writing" offensive was a corporate attack campaign, Price maintains. "The implication—and that may not be putting it strongly enough—was that MCI's telemarketers weren't telling the truth about savings."

Abandoning the Pedestal

MCI's assault on the consumer long-distance market, in essence, drove AT&T off its long-held pedestal as one of the leading corporate American icons. Before the sniping erupted with MCI, Price says AT&T was widely regarded as "nurturing, warm and genuinely interested in bringing people together." AT&T showed, however, that it could be just as aggressive at trading blows in an advertising and pricing war as its smaller rival. MCI couldn't have been more delighted.

"AT&T relinquished its pedestal and its image of being warm and nurturing to get down in the gutter to fight us for market share. We ended up scrambling up on the pedestal. While we were doing that, AT&T answered us back with their incredible fire power to tell the world why they should choose AT&T rather than MCI. It created confusion, fear and doubt, which is exactly what the monopoly competitor wants with regard to an aggressive underdog challenge."

Boiling Down a Choice

"Customers then see it as a very black-and-white choice. It's either AT&T or MCI. Sprint and the other smaller carriers are no longer in the picture. It's just us and AT&T. The No. 2 player really benefits from the public vitriol," Price contends.

"We believe that when Coke and Pepsi fight or when Anheuser Busch and Miller fight, the customers ultimately win because the pie gets bigger. And a market share battle is especially effective for the underdog because it makes the decision binary. It's either us or them." MCI focuses on taking business from AT&T, not its smaller rivals.

"Remember how John Kenneth Galbraith and William F. Buckley used to debate? They were vicious enemies. If one of them didn't exist, they would have had to invent the other because they relied on their public animosity to reinforce their images and positions. It's the same way with us and AT&T. When AT&T picks on us and we answer back, it works the same way.

"People are interested in what each of us has to say. Sometimes they are amused. They get involved because customers feel they have picked sides in a very public battle. It's like politics."

Suffering a Setback

Marketing can be as bloody as politics, as MCI found out in late 1994 when it suffered its first quarterly revenue decline in five years. In December alone, MCI lost almost 300,000 customers to AT&T.

But Price took the disappointing fourth quarter in stride. "Since we launched 'Friends and Family' in 1991, we have beaten AT&T 15 quarters to one. If we had a party every time we gained 200,000 new customers we'd have a permanent hangover. Granted, AT&T had a great fourth quarter, but the entire year of 1994 was the best we've had since the 1984 divestiture."

AT&T Chairman Robert E. Allen told shareholders at its April 1995 annual meeting that he expected more "fierce competition in the long-distance and product business. Our people aren't running for cover. We are on [the] attack."

MCI counterattacked in early 1995 by launching "New Friends and Family," which discounted prices in the popular program by another 6 percent. By spring, MCI had regained its momentum and reported a 17 percent gain in earnings for the first quarter of 1995.

While AT&T and MCI will continue to exchange advertising potshots and engage in pricing skirmishes, Price says MCI will remain focused on a target audience of young, technologically friendly people, the type of people who so enthusiastically embraced "Friends and Family."

Innovation Remains a Hallmark

Although "Friends and Family" has grown long in the tooth, it remains one of the most innovative marketing initiatives on the books. It underscored MCI's penchant for personalizing its marketing.

"I think 'Friends and Family' worked so well because it was a heck of a lot different than having a telemarketer call and say: 'You want to save with MCI?' versus: 'Hi, I'm calling on behalf of your sister Sue who has joined 'Friends and Family' and she would like you to join too.

"That way you can save money when you call her and she can save money when she calls you... and by the way, your sister says the new puppy is getting really big.' It's a whole different relationship and that's the basis of our marketing. Marketing is fundamentally about people."

Like so many underdogs, MCI has revolutionized its market. Price says MCI will continue to add new twists in its titanic battle for supremacy in the long-distance telephone market by sticking to its mantra of mobile, agile and, if necessary, hostile.

DRYPERS

If MCI's crusade to outmarket AT&T seems daunting, the current marketing challenge by Drypers Corporation is downright quixotic.

A tiny, start-up marketer of disposable diapers, Drypers has taken on the seemingly impossible mission of competing not only against Kimberly-Clark Corporation's Huggies brand, but against Luvs and Pampers, brought to you by Procter & Gamble Co.

Yet, through a combination of entrepreneurial pluck and ingenious marketing, Houston-based Drypers has made substantial headway in its drive to diaper the bottoms of the nation's infants and toddlers. It now claims 5.5 percent of the $3.8 billion U.S. disposable diaper market and vows to punch that percentage up to 10 percent.

A Window of Vulnerability

Dave Pitassi, Drypers' co-founder and managing director of marketing and sales, knew first-hand that P&G was vulnerable to a challenge from an underdog. He worked as a brand manager for P&G after graduating from college. Detecting some resentment by retailers over their thin or non-existent profit margins from the sale of premium-priced national brand diapers, Pitassi thought he could do better.

"It became clear to me that there had to be an opportunity for a smaller company when the profit margins on diapers for P&G and Kimberly-Clark were so high and the stores were often selling the products as loss leaders."

Attempting to outmarket P&G would be a tall order. With leading household brands like Cheer, Crest and Bounty, P&G is widely regarded as the world's leading marketer of consumer goods.

Nipping at the Top Dog's Heels

Nearly eight years of meteoric growth later, Drypers' $143 million in 1994 revenues is still just a drop in the bucket in comparison to P&G's $30 billion in worldwide revenue. But the top dogs know Drypers is out there nipping at their heels.

Drypers' share of market rose 10.9 percent to 5.5 percent in 1994, according to Nielsen research. P&G's share fell 3.2 percent to 34.7 percent; Kimberly-Clark's share slipped 5.8 percent to 31 percent. Private label brands rose 7.4 percent to 23.1 percent of the disposable diaper market.

P&G, which derives about 16 percent of its worldwide sales from diapers, set out to teach Pitassi and his company a lesson not long after Drypers rolled out its discount-priced diapers in 1988. Drypers' pricing strategy called for its brand to undercut the leading national brands by $1 per package.

That was until P&G flooded the market with $2-off coupons on Luvs and Pampers. So much for the price advantage. And, it was nearly so much for Drypers, recalls Pitassi from the company's sales and marketing office in Vancouver, Washington.

"We watched our cash diminishing very quickly. It was alarming. The impact was almost immediate. We weren't sure what they [P&G] were going to throw at us but we found out in a hurry," says Pitassi.

Rather than turn tail, Drypers realized its only hope for survival was to beat P&G at its own game.

Executing the 'Judo Strategy'

Drypers boldly redirected P&G's momentum and aggressive couponing against itself. Pitassi calls it the "judo strategy." It was essentially torn from the same page as MCI's "corporate jujitsu" strategy that stymied its much larger marketing adversary, AT&T.

No matter what it's called, the strategy is based on a variation of the Japanese hand-to-hand combat maneuvers that force the larger opponent to use his weight and strength against himself.

Drypers had to somehow balance the odds because it was launching product only in its home market of Houston. If Drypers diapers had been distributed in almost 70 percent of all U.S. grocery stores as they are today, it's unlikely that P&G could have afforded to focus so much of its firepower on the Houston market.

Awash With Coupons

Not surprisingly, the P&G's $2-off coupons were papering only the Houston market. "There were somewhere between $40 and $50 in diaper coupons available to the consumers at one time. It was just crazy. How do you address something like that?"

Digging in its heels for the fight of its young life, Drypers created "convertor coupons." The Drypers convertors, inserted in Sunday newspapers, stated that a Pampers $2-off coupon could be applied to the purchase of a $7.99 bag of Drypers.

The shopper had to present to the retail cashier both the Drypers convertor and the Pampers coupon. Retailers, Pitassi feared, might not accept the Drypers convertor, scuttling the program. "But the retailers accepted them with open arms. They saw us as the underdog and wanted to help."

Retailers Do Their Part

Unwittingly, retailers helped in another way. "Even if the retail cashier kept the Drypers convertor and the Pampers coupon, the two often got separated in the cash register. So where are the retailers going to send those coupons for redemption?

"They're not going to send a Pampers coupon to the Drypers Corporation. They're going to send the Pampers coupons back to P&G, which ends up paying the redemption while we get the sale."

The plan worked and thousands of new customers decided to give Drypers a try, as the spunky upstart captured about 15 percent of the Houston disposable diaper market.

'We'll Triple Your Savings'

In another gambit to counter P&G and Kimberly-Clark, Drypers created an ad whose headline stated: "Pamper, Hug and Luv Us ... Send us their coupons and we'll triple your savings."

In a typical scenario, a consumer would respond by sending in $4 worth of Pampers, Luvs or Huggies coupons. "In a sense we didn't exactly match their coupons because we would send the consumer 12 $1 coupons that could be applied to the purchase of a single package of Drypers. So the redemption diminishes, but it drives volume in the near-term.

"The majority of coupons are never redeemed because people lose them. But people get excited by them and it reinforced our image as a company that was serious about providing a high-quality, value-priced disposable diaper."

The Coupon Blitz Abates

P&G scaled back its couponing offensive, but has kept the heat on Drypers ever since through deeper everyday discounts of its Luvs and Pampers lines. In early 1995, P&G rolled back prices on Luvs and Pampers to match Drypers' average everyday retail price of $5.99.

Drypers responded by going one better. It dropped its average everyday price to $4.99. How low will things go? Drypers President and co-CEO, Terry Tognietti, would only say that "we've established a policy of not being out-valued by anyone. This decision to reduce retail prices is our way of proving to consumers and retailers that we'll do what it takes to honor that commitment."

In the late 1980's, when Drypers was fending off the coupon assault, Drypers was facing an equally dangerous marketing challenge. Brand managers from P&G and Kimberly-Clark, says Pitassi, were warning the retailers that stocking Drypers would "cannibalize" their private label brand of diapers. "Our competitors were saying: 'Go ahead and support Drypers. But all you'll do is kill your private label diapers.'

"Our response was that we were not targeting the private labels. We were clearly going after the major brands— Pampers, Huggies and Luvs. Our market was not going to come at the expense of private labels. That was not our challenge. The retailers appreciated us setting the record straight."

The Best of Both Worlds

Retailers get edgy when they detect a threat to their store brands because they traditionally enjoy higher profit margins on the private label brands. Leading brands, however, are often used as loss leaders to draw parents into their stores in hopes they'll buy other baby products like formula or baby food.

Drypers, however, could provide retailers the best of both worlds—a diaper with all the bells and whistles of leading brands, but at a lower price for the consumer and a higher profit margin for the retailer.

Unburdened by high overhead costs and Fortune 500-like layers of management, Drypers could afford to make essentially the same product for less. Everyone in Drypers' 600-member workforce wears several hats, not unlike Southwest Airlines where the same person may man the gate, load the luggage and pass out bags of peanuts on board.

Quality at a Price

"General Electric Chairman Jack Welch says the winners of tomorrow are the companies that can produce the best quality product at the lowest price. That's the operating philosophy at Drypers."

As a small company, Pitassi says it's imperative that Drypers "turn a dime into a dollar. Big companies can solve problems by spending money, not through executing creative, sometimes risky strategies.

"When you're a start-up you have no choice, because you don't have the luxury of a lot of cash," he says. "If you're smarter in promoting, smarter in manufacturing and smarter in purchasing, you're going to be able to take those proceeds and improve your quality, therefore your value is better. That is our fundamental secret."

On Turning Dimes Into Dollars

Drypers turns dimes into dollars in a variety of ways that help them compete against larger, well-heeled competitors. They include:

■ **Cooperative promotions.** Large marketers like Walt Disney Co. and Sears, Roebuck & Co. have packaged offers in bags of Drypers. "We have a very valuable commodity—the parents of infants through 3-year-olds. It's not easy to reach that target audience," says Pitassi.

"These offers, [such as] childrens' photos at Sears or discounts on baby food, benefit our consumers but also serve as a profit center for us. Advertisers who want to reach our target audience pay us a fee. The profit gives our advertising and promotions budget extra legs. We can plow the profit back into producing a quality product or apply it to the bottom line."

■ **Tightly focused advertising.** Although now a national brand, Drypers rarely advertises nationally, such as on network television. "We can't compete with P&G on a dollar-for-dollar national advertising basis. It's just too expensive," says Pitassi.

Drypers concentrates its advertising in areas where it can have the most impact: in spot TV markets, local print ads and at the point-of-purchase. Drypers in-store advertising has to be especially creative and eye-catching.

"We have to tempt the shopper to give us a look because we're not the biggest name brand. We've used shelf-talkers, sweepstakes offers, scholarships and we've hung promotional tags off the product like garment tags. It's an important opportunity to reinforce our message of value at a good price."

Drypers never strays from that central marketing message, unlike P&G and Kimberly-Clark, who must devote some of their advertising dollars to educating the market about their latest product innovations. It makes more sense to piggyback on the advertising resources of the big dogs in the market, Pitassi says.

■ **Benchmarking and reverse-engineering.** Just as Drypers is content to let P&G and Kimberly-Clark take the lead role in crowing about the latest breakthroughs in a diaper's comfort and containment, Pitassi says he is more than happy to let the competition absorb the expense of "going through the learning curve of a new product.

"We'll watch them go through the process, spend the money and develop the prototype, but we'll get to the market just as quickly. By the time we start spending to develop and market the product we're already a step ahead of them."

For example, when Kimberly-Clark introduced its disposable Huggies Pull-Ups training pants in 1990, Drypers marched out its own version several months later. Pitassi is particularly proud that Drypers, using a cross-functional product development team, was able to roll out its training pants several years ahead of P&G.

"We are research and development oriented, but we don't necessarily need to be the product pioneers to be successful," says Pitassi. "We're not like some companies who can afford to invest in research and development of a new product for five years before they make their money. We need to make money immediately on a product."

■ **Develop unique packaging.** Because it usually can't afford to pay slotting fees or allowances which manufacturers use as incentives to get retailers to display their products, Drypers reconfigured its packages to give space-squeezed retailers more flexibility.

"We were the first company to compress the diapers and the first to design our packages so that there is both a horizontal and vertical front. The retailer can stand the package up or put it on its side. And our packages have two fronts. Retailers in their schematic shelf designs now have much more flexibility. In a store, there is a lot of air space and the key is minimizing the air space. We could also proudly tell them that Drypers, far and away, could provide them the highest profit per cubic foot in the diaper category."

That argument was coupled with Drypers' contention that a regional brand really could help retailers make money instead of losing money on diapers.

"The extra effort with the packaging sent a message to the retailers that we were more mindful of their needs. We were perceived as the good guys because we were paying attention to that stuff. They noticed the extra hustle.

"Even though we couldn't pay the huge, up-front slotting fees, we sold the retailers on the idea of a longer-term business relationship. The retailers might come out a few nickels and dimes ahead with the slotting fees of the big companies, but we sold them on the idea of a long-term, day-to-day relationship that's ultimately more profitable for them."

■ **Obtain assistance from suppliers.** Drypers negotiates hard with its suppliers of such materials as tape and adhesives to get the best price. "If you can't get the supplier to give you cash discounts then you say 'Fine, can you give me a little higher quality?' There are so many ways to be opportunistic."

Drypers has turned to its suppliers for things as simple as hats and jerseys for its company softball team. "It may cost only a couple of thousand dollars to outfit and sponsor the team. It may not sound like a lot of money, but it's the principal of the thing.

"We went back to the employees and asked them who besides us could pay for uniforms and sponsorship. The answer was companies who are already selling us products. They are motivated to help us out."

Drypers' advertising agency designed and donated the caps and another supplier chipped in with uniforms. "The whole key is that the suppliers don't deduct it from what they are already doing for us. It's over and above, but it's something that builds a relationship."

A Precursor to Drypers

Drypers isn't Pitassi's first crack at running a disposable diaper company. In 1984, the then 25-year-old Pitassi and two friends from Lewis and Clark College in Portland, Oregon, launched a limited partnership called VMG Products.

Success came quickly. Unfortunately it came too quickly. Demand for the company's product outstripped supply. The only way to meet the demand was through the purchase of new equipment.

The debate over where to get the money became so bitter that the limited partners voted to fire Pitassi and his co-founders. Pitassi says he learned a lot of valuable sales and marketing lessons at VMG.

No Trial by Fire

VMG, however, was never confronted with the couponing challenge from larger competitors that served as Drypers' baptism by fire. "P&G's and Kimberly-Clark's attitude back then was, 'These guys are too young. They will kill themselves.'

"But the second time we launched against them, it was a different story. They threw legal stuff at us, the coupons, everything they could think of."

Regrouping after the initial defeat, Pitassi and his partner Wally Klemp struggled to patch together enough money to start a second company. Nearly $2.5 million was raised through venture capital and a $500,000 investment from the owner of a Portland grocery store.

Initially known as Veragon Corp., the company changed its name to Drypers to better play off the name and the nature of the product.

Launching in the Lone Star State

Up and running by 1988, Pitassi and Klemp recruited Terry Tognietti, an operations specialist from—where else but—P&G. (Tognietti, Klemp and Raymond Chambers are co-CEO's of the company.) Drypers launched in Houston because of the proximity to key suppliers and the potential for rapid growth in the Houston market.

By concentrating its initial efforts in a single market, Pitassi says Drypers could more easily focus on understanding the needs of its retailers and their consumers. The intense curiosity about those key audiences continues today but on a much broader scale.

"We communicate constantly with our customers. We collect data, conduct focus groups, we use every form of research available. I go to the stores and observe what the customers are doing. I talk to them to find out what's important to them."

Relying on Gut Instinct

"But by the end of the day we throw all that stuff out the window and make a gut level decision about what's best. Common sense will tell you that we simply have to do a better job than our competitors."

Using a brokered sales force, the company has since expanded nationally and is now selling in Asian and Latin American markets like Mexico and Argentina.

"Our sales brokers are very motivated to bust their tails to beat the direct sales forces of P&G and Kimberly-Clark." As if beating the big competitors isn't incentive enough, Drypers fires up its brokered sales reps with cash and trips to luxury destinations as rewards for stellar sales performances.

The Importance of Attitude

"Attitude is everything," says Pitassi. "I believe that if you have the right attitude you can do just about anything and that includes competing with a company many times your size."

Drypers has never abandoned the war room footing it's been on since the days of the couponing assault in the late 1980's. "We have to be ready for anything and be able to quickly respond to it," says Pitassi. Even though Drypers has diminished its risk by selling product in national and international markets, the threat remains quite real.

Facing down a common enemy is one of the important advantages of an underdog marketer.

Tested by Battle

"The best thing that can happen to any organization that may be somewhat dysfunctional is a war, because the disorganized bands have to work together. Otherwise, they are conquered. The competition of battle makes for a stronger organization." Pitassi is fond of the saying of American patriot Nathan Hale who warned his fellow revolutionaries that they'd better "hang together or they'll hang apart."

Pitassi sees his role today as a mixture of motivational speaker, coach and military leader. "If I show a lot of energy and commitment, our employees are overcome by it. There is a magnetism to the enthusiasm of a leader that draws people in and wants to make them a part of it.

"Employees need to share the company's vision," says Pitassi, who adds he'll never be intimidated by the task of facing off with competitors like P&G and Kimberly-Clark.

"Pressure makes diamonds," he says.

VIRGIN ATLANTIC AIRWAYS

Marketing dogfights are not uniquely American. If the spat between Virgin Atlantic Airways and British Airways is any measure, the British wage their turf battles with even more alacrity and vengeance.

There's been little display of British gentility in the bid for transatlantic airline passengers by British Airways, the world's most profitable airline, and Virgin, described by the *Economist* as "probably the most admired small airline in the world."

At stake are the lucrative transatlantic routes between London and U.S. gateways such as New York, Boston, Los Angeles, Miami and San Francisco. Stately British Air has the upper hand on London to New York, but Virgin, its frisky nemesis, has claimed nearly 25 percent of that traffic. That's more than both United Air Lines and American Airlines, which also compete for New York-to-London passengers.

Waging a Bitter Battle

The war of words between the two airlines often spills onto American soil. In the spring of 1995, for example, the headline in a British Airways ad stated: "More people choose British Airways to London than any other airline." The ad ends with the word "Duh" as if to suggest that British Airways' claim of superiority was self-evident.

Virgin retaliated with a two-page spread in the *New York Times*. On one page was a reprint of the British Air ad. The headline on the opposite page stated: "More people switch to Virgin Atlantic from British Airways than from any other airline. Ha!"

If words like "duh" and "ha!" hardly sound literate and proper enough for the British, consider the alleged whispering campaign British Airways waged against Virgin Airways, a piece of British billionaire Richard Branson's $2 billion empire.

British Pays the Price

Employees of $10 billion British Air engineered a smear campaign against Virgin, spreading rumors that the airline was about to fold and persuading passengers to fly with them. With doubts about Virgin's solvency, Boeing and Airbus Industries were reluctant to sell or lease aircraft to the airline founded in 1984.

Matters got very personal. Former British Air Chairman Lord King of Wartnaby ridiculed the 44-year-old Branson as "too old to rock and too young to fly."

Virgin sued for libel and British Air in 1993 was forced to apologize in a British courtroom. In addition to the very public *mea culpa,* British Airways was ordered to pay Virgin nearly $1 million in damages.

The legal battles between the two British airlines are far from over. In early 1995, a U.S. District Court judge ruled that Virgin may pursue an antitrust case against British Airways, which it claims is attempting to monopolize UK-US air passenger services. British Airways says the matter will be dismissed in due course.

A Thorn in the Side

No one at Virgin will deny that it enjoys being a thorn in British Airways' side, says David Tait, Virgin's original employee and now executive vice president. Tait, who runs Virgin's operations on the U.S. side of the Atlantic, says Virgin has never been intimidated by the size and majesty of British Air.

"Our biggest advantage in the marketplace is our smallness. British Airways' biggest disadvantage is its size. They're like the QE2, which requires a stopping distance of three miles.

"We're convinced we can do everything better than they can, except spend vast amounts of money on advertising." Because its larger rival spends about 10 times more in advertising, Virgin has to be crafty about its marketing expenditures, according to Tait.

Throwing the Rival Off-Balance

Virgin has employed a variety of underdog marketing strategies to keep its rival off balance. They include:

■ **Launch a raid on the top dog's best customers.** In a bold marketing ploy, Virgin sent direct mail to names obtained from a list broker of people who frequently fly overseas.

Virgin invited people on the list who were members of British Air's frequent flyer program to send them the original copy of their most recent statement.

In exchange, Virgin awarded respondents who had logged 50,000 miles or more on British Airways with 50,000 frequent flyer miles on Virgin—enough to fly roundtrip from the U.S. to London in economy class.

Virgin was flooded with the frequent flyer statements of thousands of British Air's most valuable customers. "We now had their names, their addresses, their most recent flight, and what class of seating they traveled in. From there, we could direct a very targeted, successful marketing campaign," says Tait.

■ **Offer a menu of quirky, hard-to-match services.** Virgin calls its business class seats "Upper Class." And with good reason.

Passengers are treated to free on-board shoulder massages and manicures, and not by the flight attendants but by professional masseurs and manicurists. The seats are roomier and each armrest is equipped with a video screen which allows the passenger to play a vast selection of movies or other programs. Virgin is even exploring the possibility of offering in-flight gambling if the U.S. Department of Transportation gives the OK. Virgin offers all this at business-class prices, which are less than British Air's first-class seats.

Another unusual amenity for upper-class passengers is free limousine service at both origination and destination airports. "Some people might say that's no big deal because if a company is going to spend $4,000 to send somebody roundtrip to London they're not going to have to take the bus to the airport," says Tait. "And that's true. So why should we bother with it?

"The reason is that we take responsibility for getting the passenger to and from the airport. It's one less thing they have to worry about. If you fly back into JFK on a rainy Friday night at rush-hour and your company limousine is not there or if your company has changed services and you can't remember, you're out of luck.

"With British Airways or the other airlines, the passenger is on his own. You can look at service two ways. Some companies ask: 'What's the least we can give our passengers and get away with it?' versus airlines that ask: 'What's the most we can invest and still make money?' "

Services that go above and beyond the call also serve to make the competition look bad, says Tait. Because British Airways flies from about 16 U.S. gateways to Virgin's seven, it's more expensive for British Airways to match the value-added services.

"If British wants to match us, they have to do it in all U.S. gateways rather than just the ones where they compete with us. They don't want to field calls from customers asking why they only get special services in cities where Virgin operates."

The amenity that takes the cake is Virgin's $1.5 million lounge for its upper class passengers at London's Heaththrow Airport. It's a road warrior's dream with laptop computers, fax machines, copiers and telephones arranged on antique desks.

Travelers can unwind by playing chess in the lounge's wood-paneled library graced by a 17th century oak table crafted from a Spanish galleon. A well-appointed salon pampers passengers with complimentary haircuts, shampoos or makeup sessions. A music room is equipped with state-of-the-art stereo equipment and stocked with Branson's private collection of compact disks.

■ **Use a limited advertising budget shrewdly.** With only $10 million to spend in the U.S. cities Virgin serves, it must get the most bang for its buck. Television advertising, the most expensive form of media, doesn't fit that description.

TV, which had been used on a limited basis in the past, is only used when Virgin inaugurates service in a new gateway city. About half of Virgin's U.S. ad budget goes into radio advertising, making it the predominant medium.

The radio spots heard during drive-time hours often use humor to reach business travelers. Virgin has used comedic British actress Tracy Ullman to humorously underscore the advantages of flying in Virgin's upper-class seats.

In addition to some print advertising in travel publications, such as *Conde Nast Traveler* and *Gourmet* magazine, Virgin has been using direct mail, which Tait likes because it can speak more intimately to customers and prospects.

"Before the frequent flyer programs came along, airlines didn't know who their customers were. They were spending the big TV dollar to reach people who were already their customers. Why resell the product to a customer you already had?

"We'd rather spend money reaching people we know are in the market for services, but who haven't been using us. We've used some very specific direct mail lists to reach people who have been to London lately."

Because its budget is so limited, Tait says Virgin has to be innovative. "The most effective advertising is the kind that's believable. So much airline advertising is not."

Airline advertising, which Tait says takes itself too seriously, typically shows "a passenger luxuriating in a misty paradise at 35,000 feet feasting on a gourmet meal. We all know that's not true. It's no wonder people have such deep suspicion about advertising."

Because Virgin can create so little noise in the market with its tiny advertising budget, the airline's messages must be fresh and different-sounding. Entertaining ads stand a far better chance of getting people's attention than the staid run-of-the mill variety. Even more important than an entertaining message, however, is a credible product to sell.

"If you've got a good product, it speaks for itself. Coming up with a good product is easy. Getting the word out is hard to do and that's why word-of-mouth is so important to a smaller company," says Tait. "It's the best form of endorsement. People tend to believe the person in the next office when he says, 'Hey, this airline is great.' Not so with advertising, no matter how good it is.''

Virgin's quirky services help create a buzz, which carry far more weight than media advertising, he believes.

■ **Launch pre-emptive strikes.** Several years ago, when Virgin learned that the major carriers were meeting with video recorder manufactures to create seatback screens on airlines, Virgin beat the big dogs to the punch.

Virgin purchased boxloads of hand-held Sony Walkman Video players and passed them out to passengers in all classes of seating. Passengers were then allowed to choose from an extensive list of movies they could watch on the flight.

"We got the jump on our competitors by several years. In a sense we lead the industry from the rear. That's the beauty of being small. You can react very quickly. It's easier to wield David's slingshot than Goliath's heavy metal sword.''

The pre-emptive strike not only won Virgin some points for innovation, but it allowed the airline to gauge its passengers' reaction to the new in-flight entertainment devices. Only after determining it was a service that passengers welcomed did Virgin undertake the expense of installing individual video screens in every seat of its fleet.

Its newer planes have been equipped with a $19 million, 14-channel, interactive entertainment system. Unlike its competitors', the in-flight system is available in both economy and upper class seating, notes Tait.

Virgin passengers had not been asking for the service in focus groups, one-on-ones or surveys, but once they were given the option of viewing an individual movie, demand was there, says Tait. "A majority of people responding to our surveys said personal, in-flight entertainment was not a factor in their selection of an airline. Most said all they wanted to do was work and sleep.

"We listened to what they had to say, but quite often the consumers don't know what they want. You almost have to spoon feed it to them. But if you're right, you gain an enormous advantage over competitors."

■ **Keep overhead low.** Virgin's overhead is about 25 percent less than British Air's. Even with its modest growth plans, Virgin only anticipates flying from 12 to 14 routes, a fraction of what British Airways flies. The lower operating costs allow Virgin to survive the bruising competition with the larger airlines that must service a vastly larger network of gateways with a huge fleet of aircraft.

Virgin's lean operation and limited routes fly in the face of conventional wisdom that says only large, global airlines, which enjoy economies of scale, will prosper. And Virgin has survived without having to go the no-frills route of Southwest Airlines.

"We provide more passenger space and more extras. What we get in return is a greater load factor and a higher following," says Tait. In its marketing, Virgin emphasizes its profitable upper class seats, which enjoy load factors of about 85 percent.

"Our prices are the same as British Airways and the other transatlantic carriers. No one can afford to price differently because fare advantages are immediately matched in this industry.

"Because we have to compete with British Airways on something other than price, differentiation of service becomes even more important. Passengers quickly ask: 'If the price is the same, then what more can I get with this guy rather than the other guy?'"

Virgin couldn't possibly afford to differentiate its service if its overhead was the same as British Airways. With apologies to Gertrude Stein, Tait says "We've never believed that an airline, is an airline, is an airline."

■ **Cultivate a hip, irreverent personality.** The Virgin name, which is better known in Great Britain where the name is on entertainment megastores, colas, vodka and computers, carries some weight in the U.S.

"The Virgin name is gaining awareness all over the world. It's a wonderful name because it's different and innovative," says Tait. Apparently not satisfied with taking on mighty British Airways, Branson launched Virgin Cola against the world's most powerful brand—Coca-Cola.

Rattled by the challenge, Coca-Cola launched a campaign in 1994 to remind Brits that Virgin is not the "real thing." Despite Coke's efforts to checkmate the upstart, Virgin Cola has captured 15 percent of the British cola market.

A flair for the dramatic can also help reinforce a maverick brand. When Virgin inaugurated new service in 1994 from London to Hong Kong, Richard Branson alighted from the Airbus 340 dressed as a pseudo Chinese emperor. The whole world was watching and laughing.

Extending the Virgin Name

The Virgin name is also being licensed to two franchisees that fly from London to Athens and from London to Dublin. When successful, franchising can provide extra revenues with minimal risk or investment; but the brand can be at risk if franchisees are sloppy about maintaining standards.

The Virgin name will be carefully nurtured, assures Tait, who admits that he thought the Virgin name would never work for an airline.

"I told Richard he must be crazy. What a ridiculous name. It will never fly," Tait recalls of his first conversation with Branson in 1984. The British-born Tait, who directed Sir Freddie Laker's North American sales operations, was an aviation industry consultant in Miami when he was approached about starting an airline.

A Name With More Panache

Initially, the new airline was going to be known as British Atlantic. But the proposed name was changed to Virgin Atlantic when Branson got involved.

"I had never heard of Branson nor Virgin for that matter

because I've lived most of my life in the United States. I later found a couple of records on the Virgin label at my home. (Branson founded the Virgin Record label at age 21. He sold it for $900 million in 1992, pocketing a $515 million profit.)

"I now realize why my career in aviation consulting never took off. Richard apparently liked my bluntness and my stubbornness because he hired me to make it work.

"There's no question that if we had been known as British Atlantic Airways with exactly the same product as British Airways we'd not be as successful. There's a lot of cachet to the name. The Virgin name is becoming widely recognized as a brand that is innovative and not afraid to challenge established brands."

A Struggle for Profits

The Virgin name, however, does not guarantee profitability. The airline failed to turn a profit in 1992, earned a small profit in 1993, but slipped back into the red in 1994 despite record revenues of $750 million. Branson, one of the richest people in Britain, was forced to lend $50 million of his own money to cover the shortfall.

Virgin, Tait predicts, will report a healthy profit by the end of 1995 for several reasons:

- High load factors, particularly on profitable upper class seats.
- Increased revenue from such new routes as San Francisco to London or London to Hong Kong.
- New, more fuel-efficient Boeing 747-400's and Airbus 340's to replace its fleet of Boeing 747-200's.
- A joint marketing or "code-sharing" agreement with Delta Air Lines, America's third-largest airline.

Approved by the U.S. Department of Transportation in February, the $200 million agreement lets Virgin sell blocks of seats to Delta at wholesale prices. Delta can then market the Virgin seats at retail prices through its extensive marketing network.

Delta will buy about 200,000 seats this year on its U.S. to London flights—nearly a quarter of Virgin's total. It's a welcome new stream of revenue. In exchange, Delta gains access to London's Heathrow Airport, the busiest airport in Europe.

Remaining Forever Aggressive

Virgin's relationship with Delta will not temper the siege mentality that drives its aggressive marketing, Tait assures. "Our slingshot is always ready," says Tait, who knows Virgin will always be on British Airways' radar screen.

"If you're doing what you're doing very well, there's no way it won't attract the attention of the industry giant. You don't even have to be stealing huge amounts of business from them because they'll notice. And when they do, you'd better be ready."

THE PRINCETON REVIEW

You would think that an organization with a name as distinguished-sounding as The Princeton Review would never get involved in an ugly, bare-knuckles brawl with a competitor. Guess again.

John Katzman, TPR's outspoken founder and president, feels nothing but contempt for his larger, more established arch rival, Kaplan Educational Centers (KEC). He's not been shy about expressing his feelings toward KEC, an $80 million unit of the Washington Post Company. He once ordered the taunt: "Friends don't let friends take Kaplan" used in an ad.

The two test-prep industry leaders help high school and college students bone up for standardized tests such as the Scholastic Aptitude Test (SAT), Graduate Record Examination (GRE) or the Medical College Admissions Test (MCAT).

Designing a Challenge

Princeton is Katzman's alma mater and it's there that it first occurred to the architecture major that students could be better prepared for the tests that can make or break their future. "I figured if nobody was doing a very good job at it there must be a market for it," says the scrappy Katzman.

His hunch was right. By 1995, his idea for a test-prep business had become a $50-million-plus enterprise with 65 offices in such places as Tokyo, Mexico City, Madrid and Lahore, Pakistan. Upstart TPR had captured twice Kaplan Educational Centers' market share in the all-important SAT segment and landed the first test-prep book ever on the *New York Times* Bestseller List, *Cracking the System: The SAT.*

TPR, which launched the first of its 45 titles in 1985, is second only to Barron's Educational Series in the test-prep book market. Kaplan Educational Centers didn't publish its first book until 1993.

Stepping in Harm's Way

TPR's success didn't go unnoticed by KEC, the industry's top dog, which has been preparing students for standardized tests since 1938. Although TPR has the edge in the SAT prep-test, KEC remains the leader in the graduate and professional prep-test market. The graduate and professional school test market combined is larger than the SAT market, according to Katzman.

"TPR's battle with KEC started with a couple of their rude ads and escalated from there," says Katzman, who got in KEC's face with some rude ads of his own. He even used the Internet to invite customers to post disparaging stories about KEC.

The two companies have not only swapped harsh words in print and in cyberspace, but in the courtroom, as well. Together, the companies have spent nearly $500,000 in legal fees suing each other over claims of false or misleading advertising. Both sides have agreed to scale back test-score improvement claims in their advertising, but other matters were still in arbitration in the spring of 1995.

Sniping Draws Attention

The long-running war of words has generated plenty of national and local press, which is one way for an underdog to get on the map, says Katzman. He warns that companies that want to trade barbs with a competitor had better have the stomach for it. That's never been a problem for Katzman, although he notes, "Frankly, I think both sides are getting tired of it."

The noisy dogfight actually has had little to do with TPR's marketing strategy, however. Its customer service, innovative, leading-edge application of technology, strategic alliances and entrepreneurial hustle in the face of a deep-pocketed competitor have driven TPR's success, according to Katzman, whose feisty company is growing nearly four times as fast as Kaplan Educational Centers.

"Don't pick fights you can't win. There are certain places where large companies have an advantage, such as advertising. They can out-advertise an underdog. The second area is litigation. They can outspend you in court. The third area is price. The bigger companies can keep their prices down until you are gone.

"Pick the fights you know you can win. For smaller companies that often means innovation, speed to market or customer service," says Katzman. TPR's most important weapons in its scrap with KEC are:

■ **Well-tuned customer service.** TPR puts fewer students in its classes than does KEC, which allows more individualized attention to be given to attending students. Average class size for graduate school tests is 12 students; 10 for the SAT. TPR's intensive, six-week classes cost about $700.

In response, KEC has lowered its average class size. Says TPR's Katzman, "Their response has been funny. They do everything we do, but they just do it a little worse. They're always second, so we're afraid they are going to leapfrog us, but they always come in with something watered down."

Katzman contends that, beginning with the first phone call, TPR differentiates its service from KEC's. "You would find that the call is handled more personally and is more focused on your needs, or your son's or daughter's. That's a critical place to win, right from the start. We don't wait until we get someone in the classroom," says Katzman.

In addition to keeping its class size intimate, TPR schools its young, dynamic instructors on the principles of customer service. "We follow up carefully with the students to determine that they not only liked the course, but liked the instructor, as well. We use surveys and follow-up telephone interviews. This is a word-of-mouth business and we want students saying good things about us to other students."

TPR says it helps about 65,000 student a year cram for standardized tests for admission to college and graduate and professional schools.

■ **Smart use of technology.** The new electronic tools of marketing and communications can help level the playing field when an underdog is facing a larger competitor, says Katzman. The trick is getting wired first.

"We have linked all of our offices with e-mail. I still don't think they have e-mail. We were about the 200th company on the Internet's World Wide Web with a home page. Our web site gets more hits in a month than they have gotten since they launched their page a year ago," says Katzman, who says the site attracts about 40,000 visitors a month. He wouldn't venture a guess as to how many of the inquiries are converted into sales, but says the home page has become an important new marketing tool for the company.

TPR also has sites on America Online and E-world, two commercial on-line services. TPR's America Online site, for example, offers students advice on how to produce a well-penned application essay, a classified advertising section where students can buy or trade products or services, and a question-and-answer section that sets the record straight about the perception that TPR only teaches test-taking "tricks."

"The Princeton Review is a serious course for students willing to work hard to improve their scores," states TPR. "We thoroughly review those topics covered on the tests for which we prepare students. Our 'tricks' are nothing more than test-taking techniques that make everyone a good tester."

The acquisition of desktop publishing technology has given TPR's marketing and testing documents a sharper edge. Computerized scanners in every office allow TPR to more quickly grade and analyze students' tests. The students appreciate the instant feedback. "It took Kaplan five or six years to catch up with our use of optical scanning devices.

"In all of those ways we use technology as a way of getting a competitive edge," says Katzman. "We only use technology as necessary and where it gives us an edge. We don't use technology for technology's sake."

■ **Striking strategic alliances.** TPR, Katzman believes, could not have grown as quickly as it did without a little help from some partners. These include franchisees, which operate about 40 of TPR's 65 worldwide offices.

TPR teamed up with publishing giant Random House to produce the best-selling *Cracking the System* series of books that prep students for all the major standardized tests.

"We're now selling more than a million books a year. It's been a steady contributor to our revenues," says Katzman. "The books reach a different market because not every student can afford a $700 course, but they can afford a $15 book. They can get a lot out of it if they work hard and stay focused."

TPR joined forces with LYRIQ International Corporation, maker of educational and entertainment software, to develop "The Princeton Review SAT Computer Diagnostic Exam." The software lets students practice for the SAT on their personal computers. It automatically scores and analyzes full-length sample exams.

Educational Testing Service (ETS), which develops and administers standardized tests, plans to replace the pencil-in-the-dot forms with exams taken on PC's.

Striking an alliance with Adam Robinson, a highly regarded

tutor in New York, gave TPR an early boost. "In the early days when I was by myself, I ran an ad saying that my SAT prep-test was producing the best results in New York City. I got a call from Adam Robinson, who told me his results were just as good as mine. I said I had the best results of any 'course'; [Robinson wasn't] a course but a tutor." Rather than split hairs, Katzman told him, "I've heard so much about you. I would like to meet you." The two broke bread over lunch and have been working together ever since.

Katzman and Robinson have co-authored the *Cracking the System* series and Robinson has developed many of TPR's best test-taking techniques.

"I could never have competed as effectively as I have without finding allies," Katzman adds.

Avoiding Pricing Skirmishes

TPR doesn't attempt to go blow-for-blow with KEC on the advertising or the pricing fronts.

"We actually try to charge a little more than Kaplan. I believe that you can't win on price as an underdog. It's a disaster because the big companies will happily lose money until you go away."

KEC, he says, relies on the deep pockets of its parent to subsidize a string of money-losing performances. "They've lost something like $30 million over the last three or four years," says Katzman. The Post Company doesn't break out financials for KEC, but the division for which Kaplan Educational Centers are a major element has reported $15 million in losses in recent years.

The Leader Sets the Price Floor

KEC's pricing strategy actually works to TPR's advantage. Barring a vicious price war, KEC's prices set the industry standard that TPR uses as a base from which to charge its slightly premium price. "People will pay more for better service," says Katzman. "Price is a very short-term way of competing. It's quality service, not price, that people talk about."

TPR, by Katzman's estimate, spends about half of what KEC spends on advertising. "We spend about $4 million to $5 million a year, but that includes producing and mailing course schedules. Our ad spending is very focused."

TPR advertises in only a few national publications and does so only in special issues such as *U.S. News'* "Best Graduate Schools" edition or *Money*'s "Best Colleges" edition. Most of TPR's ad budget is used to buy pages in high school and college publications. Its presence in cyberspace is also an effective marketing tool.

Blasting the Test Services

Although it has used its advertising to blast KEC, TPR saved some of its best shots for ETS, developer of the standardized tests. "Kaplan is at least trying to help kids, but ETS and other testing companies are actively trying to corrupt our testing system."

Katzman argues that the testing companies should be measuring command of the high school curriculum they've been exposed to rather than the students' ability to take a standardized test. "South Carolina replaced junior year English with SAT prep because they had the worst scores in the nation. What it does is create a 'shadow curriculum.' It creates companies like us," says Katzman, biting the hands that feed him.

Launching on Borrowed Money

Katzman, who was admitted to Princeton on the strength of his combined SAT score of 1500 out of a possible 1600, has long prided himself as a champion of students rights. He knows his target audience. After graduating from Princeton in 1981, he abandoned his short-lived career as a computer programmer on Wall Street, borrowed $3,000 from his parents and began tutoring 15 high school students in his parents' New York apartment.

A year later, he moved into a two-bedroom apartment in New York. "One bedroom was the Review and the other was me." TPR has since moved to a Manhattan high-rise, but Katzman still lives in the apartment.

His business grew steadily but quietly through the late 1980's. The inroads TPR was making against KEC, purchased by the Washington Post Company in 1985, went largely ignored until 1991. That's when the Washington Post Company assigned Jonathan Grayer, a young Harvard MBA, to start shaking things up at complacent and overconfident KEC.

Firing up the Troops

KEC's new-found aggressiveness only fueled the competitive fires of Katzman, and his 250 full-time employees and 6,000 part-time instructors in their mission to beat the big dog at its own game. As MCI does so effectively in its battle with AT&T, Katzman boosts his team's morale by reminding them that the market leader is trying to take a big bite of their business. "Let's say we've been energized by hating Kaplan."

TPR, says Katzman, is careful not to be blinded by its intense dislike for its rival when mapping its long-term marketing strategy. "We try our best to compete hard in whatever we are doing. But we are driven by what makes the most sense for our company."

TPR will "continue exploring the synergies between the different media that we teach in: classes, tutoring, on-line services, software and books. They are not separate universes."

Katzman's advice for an underdog under assault: "Play your game, not theirs. Whatever changes we make in our strategy is in response to what the market wants, not what Kaplan is doing."

MURIEL SIEBERT & CO.

Muriel Siebert has challenged the notion that Wall Street should be a gentlemen's club. As head of a discount brokerage bearing her name, she has taken on Charles Schwab, the nation's largest discount brokerage house.

She was one of the first to challenge the conventional wisdom on Wall Street that junk bonds and derivatives were smart money. Now, she's daring a new breed of competitors called, "superdeep discounters," to come clean.

In short, Muriel "Mickie" Siebert loves a challenge. Her penchant for rocking the boat and questioning the practices of Wall Street have helped this underdog marketer build a company that currently claims $20 million in revenues, 70 employees, and branches in Florida and California.

Her outspokenness has won her respect and attention on Wall Street, where in 1967 she became the first female member of the New York Stock Exchange. Today, Muriel Siebert is the oldest and largest woman-owned Wall Street-based securities firm.

That distinction has hardly made her complacent. Her business remains as scrappy as ever. A headline bannered across the top of the *New York Times* Money section in November, 1994, read: "Muriel Siebert's Declaration of War."

Read the Fine Print

The story was based on her ad campaign in *The Wall Street Journal* and *Investors Business Daily* that warned investors to read the fine print when doing business with the increasingly popular superdeep discounters. "Honesty and integrity should never be discounted," stated one of the headlines in the campaign, that included television spots on CNBC and local stations in New York.

Although the ads didn't specifically identify the superdeep discounters, the campaign aimed to set the record straight on how discounters can live on commissions as low as $25 to trade up to 1,000 shares of $25 over-the-counter stock. What the superdeep discounters don't make on commissions, some of them can make by "marking up" the price of the stock at the expense of the investor, says Siebert.

The campaign, says Siebert, generated a round of threatening calls from some of the superdeep discounters who dismissed her claims as sour grapes. "But I don't see how some of these new discounters can afford to charge the rates they're charging. I know the costs in this business," says Siebert, who points out that some of the aggressive upstarts require customers to have margin accounts whether they want one or not.

"When you sign on for a margin account, that gives the brokerage the right to loan out your stock and make extra revenue on it. A lot of investors buy stock for cash and do not want their stock loaned out." Muriel Siebert & Co. does not require its customers to open margin accounts.

The Authorities Take a Closer Look

Her efforts to call attention to the "disgraceful" practices of some of the superdeep discounters captured the attention of the Securities and Exchange Commission, which has taken a harder look at the superdeep discounters' advertising claims.

The television spots in the Muriel Siebert campaign referred to superdeep discounters as "untested Johnny-come-latelies with low-ball rates, unexpected charges and restrictions." The campaign also took aim on her larger, more established rivals like Schwab, Fidelity Brokerage Services, and Quick & Reilly. The spots noted that her company's pricing was 70 percent less than Schwab's and consistently less than Quick & Reilly's and Fidelity's commission rates.

"The campaign also explained that we offer all the free services of the larger discount brokerages, as well as the fact that we have more than $50 million in insurance on our accounts, which is more than Quick & Reilly has."

The transaction cost for 1,000 shares of $25 over-the-counter stock at Siebert is about $50 versus $155 for a similar transaction at Schwab.

In addition to price, Muriel Siebert tries to beat the Big 3 discount brokers in two other ways:

■ **Customer service.** "Customers like to be known," says Siebert. "They appreciate the personal attention and like the fact that a senior officer of the firm is available at all times if they have a complaint or question. A senior officer is always posted on our trading desk."

Schwab, she notes, opens up about a quarter of a million accounts every three months, while her firm has only about 80,000 active accounts versus 3.1 million for Schwab. "At which firm do you think you'll get more personal attention?" Siebert asks. A big discounter will lend an ear to its customers' concerns, but it's unlikely that person will be a senior officer, who naturally has more authority to get things right.

One of the big advantages of being a smaller firm is that "people trust us," she adds.

■ **Quality of the execution.** "We think ours is the best in the business," says Siebert. "We're right here in the heart of Wall Street. We can execute a trade the moment a customer wants it. It's something we're very careful about."

Winning High Marks

It's that kind of careful attention to detail and the customer's needs that Siebert believes helped her company rank ahead of Schwab, Fidelity and Quick & Reilly in *Smart Money* magazine's annual rating of the nation's discount brokerages. In the rankings published in the July 1995 issue, Muriel Siebert was ranked fourth (up from seventh in 1994) among the nation's leading discount brokers. Schwab was No. 6; Fidelity, No. 8; and Quick & Reilly, No. 12. The No. 1 firm was Jack White.

According to the magazine, Muriel Siebert tied for first in two of the 10 categories used to rank the brokerages: "staying out of trouble" and "quality of automated transactions." The firm also received high scores for levels of service, breadth of products and broker training.

Acting Affirmatively

As a woman-owned firm, Muriel Siebert has taken advantage of affirmative-action programs that have allowed her company to compete with large Wall Street firms that have long monopolized public finance underwritings.

Each year, Siebert has won 30 to 40 spots in underwriting syndicates for municipal bond business. In 1993 alone, Siebert underwrote pieces of bond issues totalling about $19 billion.

Marketing Goodwill

To attract that kind of business, she devised the Siebert Entrepreneurial Philanthropy Plan or SEPP. Under the plan, Siebert gives a percentage of the profits her firm earns from the underwritings to a charity in the issuing community. For example, a portion of the profits made from underwriting a New York City debt issue is funnelled back into a social service organization in the city.

In the past five years, Siebert has donated nearly $4 million to charities through SEPP. Although SEPP is not a marketing program, *per se,* the attention the program has generated has translated into more business. "It's something unique and gets us remembered. I think it also says we care about the communities in which we're participating in bond underwritings."

A Rapid Rise on Wall Street

Mickie Siebert has been doing things differently since she hit Wall Street. After dropping out of Case Western Reserve University in her native Cleveland, at age 22, she landed a $65-a-week job as a researcher at Bache Co. (In 1981, Prudential acquired Bache.) She admits that she lied that she had a college degree to get the job.

Her lack of a diploma, however, didn't inhibit her success at Bache, where she rose to the rank of senior analyst. She later became a partner at three small Wall Street investment firms; but it was the top job at a firm she was after. She was advised that, in order to get it, she'd have to start her own firm, which would require that she have a seat on the New York Stock Exchange, an institution that had never had a woman as a member.

On December 28, 1967, Siebert bought her seat on the NYSE for $445,000. Siebert, who had been earning $300,000 a year, had no problems affording the seat. The more serious problem was her lack of acceptance on the Big Board.

"I ran into a lot of hostility the first couple of years," she says. "I began to realize after a couple of years that they weren't against me on a personal basis, but more as a matter of principle. They liked things *status quo*. The men didn't feel that a woman belonged there."

There's still a lingering air of hostility toward women on Wall Street that she suspects has discouraged more women from launching entrepreneurial ventures.

"We're seeing more women starting money management firms—which is a great business—but for some reason women don't want to come in and slug it out in the brokerage field."

Seizing the Moment

Siebert proved the men wrong by "putting my head down and charging ahead." Though she had been in business since 1967, in 1970, she incorporated her sole proprietorship as Muriel Siebert & Company, specializing in research and trading stocks for institutions. Her big break came in May, 1975, when the Securities and Exchange Commission repealed rules requiring fixed commissions in the brokerage industry. "Whenever there is a change in a major law, there is a marketing opportunity. You have to seize it."

As Schwab did at the time, Siebert recast her business as a discount brokerage, charging less than half the commissions of the full-service brokerages such as Merrill Lynch. Although Schwab went on to become the Wal-Mart of discount brokerage houses, Muriel Siebert grew steadily by catering to a much smaller universe of higher net-worth individual investors and a cadre of institutional investors.

Marketing always played a key role in her company's success. "Ours is purely a marketing business. You always have to bring in new customers because by nature you are always losing customers because of deaths, marriages or the liquidation of their stocks to other people," says Siebert.

Retaining the Customers

"We also worked very hard at keeping the customers we have by performing to meet their needs. You should only sell what you absolutely know you can deliver to the customer. You have to be realistic, otherwise you have disappointed customers. And they won't be with you for long."

More than 25 years after becoming an NYSE member, Siebert has won the respect of the still heavily male-dominated Big Board. "Some of the men who were against me initially were 100 percent for me in later years."

Her years of lobbying for a women's restroom off the NYSE's seventh-floor trading room didn't succeed until 1987, when she threatened to have a portable toilet delivered to the board of directors' office. Ever the underdog, Siebert will forever delight in challenging the powers that be.

"I still very much enjoy showing the gentlemen what they've got to do," she says.

3 The Differentiators

Not all underdog marketers snipe, sue or slash prices to outmarket the competition. Unlike the Challengers of the previous chapter, the Differentiators often go quietly about their business, though they are ever mindful of what the big dogs are doing.

The companies you'll meet in this chapter are as different as the marketing strategies they use to make a profit or gain share, or both. What they all have in common, however, is a drive to do things differently than their larger competitors.

Most aim to do things more personally than their rivals do. Such is the inherent advantage of a smaller marketer, who is several layers closer to the customer and stands a far better chance of operating on a first-name basis.

Personal relationships are more resilient than those established over the television, the favored medium of the mass marketer. So long as The Differentiators keep doing things not only differently, but better, they've probably got a customer for life.

Lois Mitten, owner of a small chain of child care centers in Toledo, Ohio, realized she had to do things differently when Kinder-Care, the national chain of child care centers, showed up on her doorstep.

While on a business trip, she discovered by chance the formula that would set her apart from the national chains. Her moment of inspiration arrived while visiting a children's museum. She visited nearly a dozen more throughout the country, incorporating many of the concepts into her Children's Discovery Centers.

Home Hardware has always prided itself on being Canada's favorite neighborhood hardware store. The competitive landscape changed in a big way when Atlanta-based Home Depot moved in with its massive, warehouse-style hardware and home improvement centers.

So what did Home Hardware do to checkmate the giant discounter from south of the border? It stuck to what it does best— lavishing the customer with personal attention in the intimate confines of its corner hardware stores.

Kuczmarksi & Associates, a respected Chicago-based management consulting firm, is no threat to the ranks of the Big 6 management consulting firms. Rather than help companies roll heads in corporate re-engineerings, K&A concentrates on its speciality of helping companies become more profitable through innovation and new product development.

K&A spreads the word of its forte through what it calls expertise-based marketing, which takes the form of authoring books, delivering keynote speeches and sponsoring seminars.

Peoples Bank of Indianapolis found its turf invaded by outsiders—large, regional banks from neighboring Ohio and Michigan. Peoples cleverly parried the threat into an advantage by featuring the departing mascots of once locally-based bank in an advertising campaign.

Seizing on what bank President and CEO William McWhirter saw as the opportunity of a lifetime, Peoples raised $10 million in a public stock offering to underwrite the hiring of new personnel to write loans for businesses who still wanted to do their banking with a home-grown institution.

The Tattered Cover, Denver's legendary bookstore, has withstood the pressure of a chain bookstore invasion by serving up extraordinary customer service. Owner Joyce Meskis practically wrote the book on service in the bookstore business by making her store a community resource center and by leaving no stone unturned in quest to locate out-of-print books.

Edward D. Jones & Co. can boast that it has the most retail branches of any brokerage firm in U.S. It has one just about everywhere but Wall Street.

Jones makes its money by catering to customers on Main Street. Even though it's lately taken aim on the suburbs of large cities, the brokerage is unlikely to invite retaliatory measures from the big dogs on 'The Street.' Explains Jones' chief John Bachmann: "We're different. I don't think a firm like ours, whose investing philosophy is 'buy-and-hold,' represents any threat to them."

Finally, there's *Executive Female* magazine. It differentiates itself from other professional womens' magazines by emphasizing the executive nature of its readers.

Advertisers like reaching the well-defined and influential audience that *Executive Female* delivers. Advertisers also like a relationship that doesn't end once they've signed a contract for a page in the magazine. Marketing Director Brenda S. Ginsberg works to arrange for her readers to meet its major advertisers on a one-to-one basis.

Now, meet the Differentiators.

CHILDREN'S DISCOVERY CENTER

Lois Mitten never considered herself an underdog marketer until the day she was surprised to find two KinderCare managers walking through her Children's Discovery Center.

At the time of the visit, KinderCare, the half billion dollar national chain of daycare centers, was already operating two new sites in Toledo, Ohio, where Mitten had been quietly operating since 1982. KinderCare had opened its first Toledo center less than two miles from Mitten in 1985, and later opened another center only a half mile away.

"I was legitimately concerned, but I wasn't angry and I didn't panic," says Mitten, whose small chain has grown to five centers with total revenues of $2.5 million.

Creating Something Unique

"I talked to my accountant about how close KinderCare was coming. I wasn't sure what it would mean. I asked him: 'What should I do?' He told me that if I create something that is so unique and different then it won't matter if there are child care centers on every side of you. Parents will always choose you."

It was sage advice, for Mitten soon began developing what's been lauded as the most creative children's environments in the country. She visited a dozen children's museums throughout the country and incorporated ideas from the exhibits into her Children's Discovery Centers.

KinderCare hasn't gone away, but she's no longer looking nervously over her shoulder at what the nation's biggest daycare provider is up to. "It's important that I know what KinderCare and other competitors are doing, but I really don't focus on them. I focus on my company," she says.

Collecting Competitive Intelligence

To keep tabs on the competition, Mitten examines her publicly-owned rivals' filings with the Securities Exchange Commission. SEC documents have given Mitten a stronger sense of the demographic profile of customers they're seeking and types of locations that interest KinderCare and other publicly operated childcare rivals.

Once a year, she spends about $200 to hire a mystery shopper to scope out the competition. And while he or she is at it, the mystery shopper also drops in on the five CDC's to provide Mitten an unbiased look at her own operation. "Frankly, I don't hear much about the nearby KinderCare Centers. They are sleepers and aren't active in the local childcare community."

CDC's differentiation strategy has paid huge dividends and helps keep the big dogs at bay. Here's how she's done it:

■ **Create the best, most unique product affordable.** Struggling to create something so unique in childcare that it would become a "must buy," Mitten said she came across the children's museum idea almost by accident.

"My daughter and I were driving along a freeway in Colorado where I was doing some consulting work when she saw a sign for a children's museum. She said maybe I should stop and get some ideas. I went and quickly decided that the children's museum concept was the answer."

Collecting ideas from other children's museums throughout the country, Mitten had the formula that would allow her to stand apart from the competition.

Her three newest centers are modeled on offerings from some of the nation's best children's museums. For example, youngsters can dig for fossils and dinosaur bones in a fossil dig behind a giant dinosaur. They can climb inside a model rocket ship, speak into a whisper tube or play with an anti-gravity machine.

To give children a taste of commerce, the newer CDC's feature scale-model versions of a grocery store, a restaurant, a flower shop, a dentist's office and an accountant's office. "It allows the children to experience the real world within the safety of our world," she says.

The genuine articles donated by the business community include shopping carts, a dentist's chair and a computer.

■ **Command a premium price.** "Some people say we are too expensive, but that's all right. We know that not everyone can afford us, but for those who can, we want to make it the best possible."

Parents generally won't balk at paying a premium for the care of their children if they know it means a stronger curriculum, teachers with degrees in education or early childhood development, and a more creative environment. "I try to make it as exciting as possible for the children through a quality program. At the same time, I realize the importance of maintaining a profit in order to keep this business."

Child care operators must usually choose between serving middle to upper-middle class households or competing on price. CDC could not afford to compete on price, because it would undermine the quality of the program that makes it unique, says Mitten.

In the spring of 1995, a week's worth of care for infants was $107; for toddlers, $98; and $93 for pre-schoolers. The price includes catered lunches, two snacks and a wealth of educational materials. More than 700 children are enrolled at the centers, which also offer after-school programs for youngsters up to age 10. CDC has about 100 staff members.

■ **Keep overhead low.** Like all good underdog marketers, Mitten looks for ways to pinch pennies so she can apply the savings either to the bottom line or to marketing programs that will attract and retain customers. She pays herself only a small salary.

Instead of enjoying a salary commensurate with the head of a $2.5 million enterprise, she gets her compensation in the form of a lease payment. She owns the real estate for all five of her centers and Children's Discovery Center leases the space from her.

Although she pays the mortgage, she's building equity based on the value of the real estate. Much thought goes into site selection. "Location, location, location," the mantra of real estate entrepreneurs, is equally critical in child care. "What we look for is visibility with good highway access, lots of nearby commercial operations and an upper middle class area. The cost can be prohibitive, however."

■ **Focus marketing efforts on the best prospects.** Mitten sent 1,200 promotional videotapes to parents meeting certain demographic criteria. The tape helped announce CDC's newest center in the Toledo suburb of Perrysburg. She spent about $1,000 to buy a list of prospects from a local mailing service. Production and distribution of the tape cost an additional $14,000.

Those who received the professionally produced video lived within five miles of the new center, had children from infants through age 5, and household income of $50,000 or more. Because parents can typically only spend up to 10 percent of their gross income on child care, CDC did not target households with less than $50,000 incomes. CDC's average, full-year tuition is $5,000.

The CDC video featured testimonials from parents and highlighted its innovative curriculum and enrichment classes. Parents who watched it and brought it to the Perrysburg center within 30 days could register their child for free.

"The response was tremendous. It built a lot of awareness for us. The only problem was that we sent it out in January and parents have usually already committed their children to a school at that point. Next time, we'll do it in the spring."

Parents who took the bait and paid the new center a visit got a first-hand look at the facilities. "Once we get people in here to notice the difference, there's a much better chance of their spreading the word to other parents."

■ **Create a board of advisers.** Mitten says she has an informal board of experts to thank for some of her best marketing ideas. While large companies can afford the luxury of a salaried board of directors and expensive consultants, the entrepreneur often tries to go it alone.

"That's a serious mistake," says Mitten. "A board of advisers can make all the difference in the world. I am like a sponge. I try to drink in everything available from the business community, because I did not have a background in business." Mitten, who has a master's degree in home economics education, taught at a small college in Pennsylvania before she and her husband moved to Toledo, where he had accepted a job.

"In 1984, I established an advisory board that consists of my accountant, my attorney, my banker and an early childhood development professional from the community. We meet quarterly to review the company's performance and, many times, they have steered me away from very bad decisions and have prodded me to take advantage of growth opportunities."

She's also exposed herself to helpful marketing and management advice by serving on boards at the state and local level in both the childcare and business community. Her corporate contacts have helped her land some childcare consulting assignments.

CDC's Child Care Services Division assists small businesses, hospitals, churches and Fortune 500 companies with educational and technical expertise to address their child care needs.

Mitten is a quick study. She was honored as Entrepreneur of the Year for Northwestern Ohio in 1991. She was named the 1993 small business person of the year by the Cleveland District of the U.S. Small Business Administration.

■ **Attend seminars.** In addition to the valuable advice she's absorbed from her advisors, Mitten attends several professional development seminars throughout Ohio and the country every year. The ideas she's collected at those sessions help keep the company's marketing and product development fresh and ahead of the pack.

She's gone as far away as Italy in her quest for inspiration. Mitten and one of her employees went to Italy as part of U.S. study delegation on child care. In the Italian town of Reggio Emilia, she visited a child care center that *Newsweek* describes as the best in the world.

"At this center, their philosophy is that children should be rich and powerful and should be provided the curriculum and the space to achieve their potential. It's a philosophy we're incorporating in the training of our staff." Higher levels of training and salary for CDC teachers and staff have helped minimize turnover, which is tragically high in the child care industry, she notes.

CDC's Uncertain Start

CDC, which has been posting a nearly 25 percent growth rate in recent years, struggled in its infancy. Two years prior to launching her own business, Mitten began a small child care center at a Toledo church.

Her role there ended when the pastor told her she should look for work elsewhere, saying only that she was overqualified. Her unexpected demise at the church day care center left her with a chip on her shoulder, Mitten admits.

The chip was lifted after she was inspired by the movie "Chariots of Fire." "One of the characters, Harold Abrams, had a chip on his shoulder because he thought his university was treating him badly. He went and ran the best race of his life to prove a point."

Driven by a New Attitude

"The movie made me realize that I was given a lot of abilities by God. I decided to run my own business to the very best of my abilities. My whole attitude changed."

The pursuit of her dream got off to rocky start. Eight months pregnant, the mother of two borrowed $12,000 from a savings and loan against the equity in her home to lease a small building in a Toledo industrial park. To make matters worse, her husband had just lost his job and the couple had no insurance. Her parents were helping with the house payments.

The initial enrollment at the center was eight children, most of whom were enrolled at the church day care center she'd been asked to leave.

Suffering an Early Setback

After the birth of her third daughter, Mitten hired a substitute administrator to operate the center while she convalesced from a Caesarian delivery. Not long after returning, she was hospitalized for an infection arising from the C-section.

Her business lost $11,000 that first year, nearly the amount she had borrowed against the equity in her home. Thanks to word-of-mouth endorsements from parents, enrollment was rising, but the lack of cash was threatening the center's future.

A strong faith and a little luck helped her turn the corner. While attending a small business class at the University of Toledo, she wrote a business plan. She presented it to her instructor, who was also a local banker.

A Plan for Success

Impressed with the plan, her instructor introduced her to a loan officer who then approved a much-needed infusion of cash. Her business continued to struggle, but, after three years, she was able to buy the building she had been leasing. That was a critical turning point.

Mitten is considering franchising the Children's Discovery Center concept in other cities. The first franchise may be established in Cleveland, about two hours from Toledo.

To repay what she believes was the Lord's blessing, Mitten has incorporated a religious component in the instruction at CDC. "I wanted to teach the children that there is a God who loves and cares for them and that they need to love and care for one another."

The Role of Religion

"We read Bible stories and use that as the basis of talking about friendship and caring for one another." Mitten can recall only a handful of objections over the years from parents concerned about the religious overtones.

"Parents have been overwhelmingly in favor. Many of them are busy professional people and admit they've been lax about teaching their children about faith and moral structure. They say they appreciate our taking the time to do it. We determined early on that we in no way would attempt to prejudice the children against the faith or lack of faith of their parents.

"It's by no means the primary component, which is quality child care. But the religious influence is an element that helps differentiate us from the other centers. It's not been a negative for us, it's been a positive."

HOME HARDWARE

When Home Depot, America's largest hardware store chain, invaded Canada, Home Hardware defended its turf with a proven strategy, by reinforcing the one-to-one bond it had struck with its customers.

Home Hardware, a non-profit cooperative of nearly 1,000 dealer-owned stores throughout Canada, has prided itself since 1964 on an intimacy with the customers who walk through the doors of its 8,000-square foot stores in every province and territory in Canada.

It's the kind of customer relationship that Home Depot would find hard to replicate in its cavernous, 130,000-square-foot warehouse stores. Atlanta-based Home Depot established a beachhead in Canada with the purchase of Canada's Aikenheads chain, which in terms of square footage was the largest hardware warehouse operation in Canada.

Home Depot's tack was similar to Wal-Mart's. The American retailing giant marched into Canada by acquiring 120 Woolco stores.

All's fair in the era of free trade in North America. Still, the growing presence of huge, south-of-the-border retailers sent chills up the spines of many of Home's dealer-owners, says Al Nash, Home's retail development manager. "Any time there's new competition, there's the potential to lose business. You stand up and take notice.

"Some of our members would look at their own little location and see this big monster coming. They were convinced they were going to lose their business," says Nash. "They were saying: 'I might as well close my doors next week.' Somehow we had to allay those fears."

There were no closed stores, no margin-sapping price wars. "It would not have been a good idea to launch a price war. If we were to lower our prices, Home Depot could probably go back and lower their prices further. No one is going to win.

"You're looking at shrinking margins. That's the way national retailing is going. But you don't want to start giving things away on the top end because it erodes pretty quickly on the bottom end.

"We stuck to our long-term strategic plan and it worked," says Nash. "The first Home Depot in Canada opened up within a quarter of a mile of one of our stores. And our store is still doing very well."

Sales may slip at the Home store briefly while curious shoppers check out the new kid on the block. "But once the curiosity wanes, we do find that the consumers come back."

Home's traditional strength has been in rural Canada, where Home's fleet of bright yellow trucks ply the highways. But the rural locations have not been immune to the new warehouse operations, which tend to locate in more metropolitan areas.

"Because of the size and attractions of the warehouse centers, consumers are apt to travel farther to reach them," says Nash, noting that both the rural and metropolitan stores have faced increased competition. Home's primary target audience is the do-it-yourself homeowner. The secondary target is the building and remodeling contractor.

Home, Canada's largest independently-owned retail hardware chain with $1.6 billion in sales, keeps customers coming back several ways:

■ **Personalized customer service.** Because most dealers know the names of their regular patrons and have a habit of using them when they walk through the door, customers feel right at home. "If a dealer made one percent more a year by calling out the customer's name then we think it's well worth the effort," says Nash.

"The big thing we have going in our favor is that at Home Hardware it's still the independent retailer on the floor. It's the owner down there making sure that everything is being looked after for the customer. There's a camaraderie between the dealer and staff and the customer. Our reward is a loyal customer. That's our niche in the market."

Home's brand of customer intimacy goes beyond a friendly greeting at the door. "We have a store in Toronto that still delivers light bulbs. It's just an example of providing service to the hilt."

Customers in a hurry, particularly contractors whose time is money, prefer the compact, familiar-looking confines of a Home Hardware store versus a Home Depot warehouse. "How long will the contractor have to spend just locating a hammer and then getting through the checkout at a Home Depot? Those places can be intimidating. At a Home Hardware, he knows right where to find it. He's done and out the door."

When faced with a choice between supporting a Canadian-grown retailer or a U.S.-based concern, Nash believes consumers will tip their hats to Home. "There's a little bit of patriotism involved," says Nash. "People like to support their neighborhood store. People on the north side of the border are used to one way of doing things."

The Home Hardware name is recognized by 99 percent of the nation's consumers, making it as Canadian as hockey or the Royal Mounted Police.

■ **Guarantee the quality of the products sold.** Home has what it calls a "no quibble policy." If the customer isn't completely satisfied, the dealer will replace the product or refund the purchase price.

Under its "WE" (warranty exchange) program for small appliances and power tools, Home will exchange a defective product for a new one up to a year after it was bought.

■ **Play to your strong suit in advertising.** In its television advertising, Home makes its "camera-appropriate" dealers the star of the show. "The spots are shot right on the floor to create a little intimacy."

Customer surveys indicate they prefer commercials with genuine dealers rather than some silver-tongued spokesperson. The dealer-owners also get a charge out of having 30 seconds in the spotlight. It's not only good for the ego, but for sales, as well.

"The response from the immediate area is just phenomenal," says Nash. Home integrates all its TV, print, direct mail, catalogs, and point-of-purchase communications to deliver the same central message: "Great price and friendly advice."

Home is quick to remind consumers that its prices are competitive with the warehouse operations. "When you look at our small stores, you might think we have higher prices, but we really don't. In most cases, we're very competitive."

Perhaps in reaction to the arrival of big dogs like Home Depot and Wal-Mart, Home Hardware in 1995 incorporated into its communications the fact that it has "over 900-store buying power. We're letting people know that we can offer them good prices, because we have the strength to negotiate with suppliers. And because we are a dealer-owned company, there are no middlemen."

Although Home has a suggested retail price on everything in its 40,000-item inventory, dealers are free to call the shots on pricing merchandise in their stores. In addition to the suggested price, dealers get pricing guidance from Home's headquarters office in St. Jacobs, Ontario, where retail price points are researched in all of Canada's regions to assure competitiveness and profitability.

■ **Collect and listen to customer feedback.** Home makes extensive use of consumer focus groups to gauge how well it's serving the clientele. Surveys are also conducted, and both survey and focus groups findings are channeled back to dealers through written communications and meetings.

"We'll often pull out two or three very strong points from the results and focus on them, as well as build them into our strategic planning for the year," says Nash.

■ **Invest in training.** Because the dealer and the staff are the critical link to the consumer, Home Hardware provides a raft of training workshops, management/orientation seminars and product knowledge schools throughout the year. Full programs, including videos and manuals, are available to support in-store training.

Home's management training seminar is a comprehensive four-day session for dealers, managers and key personnel. Attendees are schooled in store and financial management, systems and services, merchandising and inventory control.

Sales training seminars are offered throughout the year. "1995 will be our strongest year ever for sales training," says Nash. More than 2,000 employees will receive some form of training in 1995. The cooperative has two full-time people who coordinate training.

■ **Assist the dealer on every front.** Because its goal is to insure the survival of the independent hardware dealer, the Home Hardware cooperative provides its members with services that go beyond advertising and training support. They include:

- Seasonal Markets. Held every spring and fall in a special, warehouse-sized facility at Home's headquarters, dealers and their staff attend this private trade show. More than 600 suppliers exhibit their products during the event.

  The Seasonal Markets also feature workshops and seminars where dealers get first-hand sales techniques and product demonstrations. Home's new advertising and marketing programs are also presented during the events, which give dealers from across Canada the chance to meet with each other, swap ideas and renew the "Home" spirit.

- Determining a location. Because this decision is so critical to the success of a retail business, Home's marketing department works closely with a dealer or a prospective dealer on site selection.

  "We do surveys and have access to market research materials so we can estimate what sales can be expected in a given area," says Nash. "That information is instrumental in establishing a location. We want a location that offers sales potential yet is affordable."

- Forecasting. Professionally prepared five-year financial forecasts based on current economic conditions and historical data on the actual performance of hundreds of similar operations give dealers insight into their stores' futures.
- Store Planning Services. Using a computer-aided design system, Home can help its dealers design or redesign the exterior and interior of their stores. The objective is to help dealers make the most productive use of their space and product layouts.
- Weekly Letter. This newsletter keeps dealers abreast of the latest information within the company. Product and service information is broken into special sections for easy reading.
- Dealer Service Hotline. Employees at Home's four distribution centers throughout Canada answer dealers' questions and help them resolve any difficulties they may encounter.

Home Hardware's cooperative structure is similar to Chicago-based True Value Hardware Stores, which also operate in Canada. Walter Hachborn, Home's founder and president, tapped True Value executives for advice on establishing a hardware cooperative in Canada.

Many independent Canadian hardware dealers in the early 1960's found they could not remain profitable by following the traditional methods of distribution. A cooperative, however, would allow them to eliminate the middleman's profit, buy products for less, and build a strong base of resources and facilities to meet any form of competition.

As a result, Home Hardware has been able to grow in the face of an enormous competitive challenge—the invasion of the giant U.S.-based warehouse stores.

Home, which also operates a chain of furniture stores, has been expanding the number of its 40,000-square-foot "Home Building

Centres." In some cases, the retailer will have to find a new site to accommodate a broader selection of hardware, plumbing, electrical, decorating and building products.

"One of our strongest opportunities lies in the existing dealer membership by encouraging them to develop into full-line building centers. The wider mix of merchandise will get the customer in and out of the stores more often. It does not provide a higher gross, but it does create higher sales volumes," says Nash.

Regardless of whether the retailer is selling in the 8,000-square foot corner store in the neighborhood or in the Building Centre five times its size, the degree of customer intimacy will remain the same, assures Nash. "That's our niche. It's that extra service that makes us different."

KUCZMARSKI & ASSOCIATES

When the big dogs do management consulting, they charge a $2 million fee to tell the corporation how to lop off $10 million in overhead. But that hypothetical example is not Kuczmarski & Associates' style of management consulting, explains Thomas D. Kuczmarski, founder and president of the Chicago-based firm. K&A's mission is not to guide a corporation through "re-engineering" or "retrenchment"—two managerial buzzwords of the 1990's.

K&A and its 30 employees are happy to leave that kind of "cost-side" management consulting to the consulting wings of the nation's Big Six accounting firms or the re-engineering consultancies that have sprouted across the corporate landscape.

"They can help a corporation streamline its operation and reduce costs and drop the profits to the bottom line. That's a nice form of consulting, because it's pretty easy for me to tell you that if you give me $2 million I'll streamline your business, eliminate some positions and save you $10 million on the bottom line. It's pretty hard to argue with $8 million in incremental profits."

Unlike the cost-side management consultants, K&A works on

the demand side. "We help companies grow by increasing the demand for their products or by stimulating demand with new consumers via new products and services. That's the first layer of differentiation," says Kuczmarski, one of the nation's pre-eminent authorities on new product and service development.

Because the competition on the demand side of the management consulting business is just as intense as it is on the supply side, K&A has to further differentiate itself. Practitioners on the demand side include research and development firms, corporate identity specialists, new product development boutiques and advertising agencies.

Specialized firms operate along the new product development spectrum, starting with strategy, exploratory research, research with customers, idea generation, concept development, and prototype development on through commercialization and launch of the product.

"An advertising agency, for example, will focus on the product's commercialization and launch through the development of the marketing and advertising campaign. That's the outer edge of the spectrum," says Kuczmarski. "We don't get involved in an ad campaign, but we do handle the first five or six steps, all the way through developing a final prototype of the product."

Corporations that assign the various new product development tasks to several specialized boutiques not only prolong the process, but run the risk that the product will be not be as well-integrated as it would if a single firm handled it, says Kuczmarski. "We provide the total chain, as opposed to a piecemeal approach."

K&A's differentiation strategy has paid off. The firm, named one of the 100 best consulting firms by respected trade publication *Consultants News,* has enjoyed a compounded annual growth rate of 35 percent a year. It can boast of a roster of Fortune 500 companies from throughout the country, and Kuczmarski fields a growing number of speaking requests from throughout the world.

K&A sets itself apart in the marketing consulting field in other ways:

■ **Focus on personal expertise rather than methodology.** "There are a lot of management consulting firms that build their reputations on the process they bring to a client. We, on the other hand, market our expertise," says Craig Terrill, a partner who heads K&A's services marketing practice.

Rather than marketing itself on the strength of a cookie-cutter methodology that can be executed by junior members of a large consultancy, K&A can offer "genuine experts in the areas of new products and services development to help clients innovate to grow profitably," he says.

"When the big firms are marketing, they don't sell their individuals because they don't necessarily have the expertise. They are experts at managing a methodology. The big firm in essence is saying: 'Trust the firm, don't worry about the people,'" says Terrill, a former manager at Andersen Consulting, the world's largest consulting firm.

"The big firms will often send a senior partner to the first meeting with a client, but it's the lower-level people just out of M.B.A. school who do all the work. The firm had better have a good methodology, because the individuals don't yet have the business acumen."

■ **Know the niche.** Although it rarely competes against his former employer, Terrill says K&A has competed for consulting contracts against such big international, independent consulting firms as McKinsey & Co., a 2,500-person demand- and cost-side specialist, and Booz Allen & Hamilton, which also has practices on both the demand and the cost side.

"That's not a problem because when you really know your niche, you have an edge over competitors that are broad and general and just swooping into the niche. The people we put in front of the client have known that niche for years versus the people they put in front of the client who may have worked in that niche only once or twice."

When the big consulting firms, both the independents and the Big Six affiliates, submit a proposal, those firms win about three times out of 10, says Kuczmarski, who was a principal at Booz Allen & Hamilton until he launched his own firm in 1983. "Our hit rate is six or seven out of 10, because we market ourselves from the perspective of experts rather than generalists."

K&A partners and associates establish their expertise by serving as keynote speakers, authoring books or writing articles for business and professional journals. In the larger firms, where the climate is more sales-driven, partners are usually required to join country clubs where they "make rain" for the firm by cultivating contacts with influential and wealthy members.

Expertise-based marketing is much more valued at K&A than relationship or "old boy" network marketing, says Kuczmarski. K&A communicates and articulates its expertise-based marketing several ways:

- Writing books. Kuczmarski's "Managing New Products: The Power of Innovation" is regarded as one of the most comprehensive treatises on developing new products. It helps establish Kuczmarski and the firm as experts in the field.

  Unlike the big consulting firms that carefully protect their methodology the way Coke guards its secret formula, K&A gives its away through the publication of books. "That's because we emphasize the expertise of our individuals rather than a secret methodology," Terrill points out. "The value is in our people."

- University teaching. Kuczmarski, Terrill and other partners are adjunct faculty members at such prestigious schools as Northwestern University's Kellogg Graduate School of Management and the University of Chicago Graduate School of Business.

  Not only does the affiliation with a major business school lend credibility, but it has exposed Kuczmarski over a period of 11 years to more than 3,000 students who are now decision-makers at their own companies and potential clients.

- Writing for business and professional journals. Articles in such industry publications as *Marketing News, Business Marketing* and the *Journal of Marketing* keep Kuczmarski & Associates in front of people in the trade.

- Public speaking. Delivering keynote addresses or lectures at major industry conferences exposes K&A to influential audiences. It's an opportunity for the firm to showcase its expertise.

- Publicity. Members of the firm are frequently cited in *The Wall Street Journal, Fortune* and *Business Week.* Because of the firm's expertise in new product development, innovation and marketing strategy, reporters are quick to turn to K&A for a quote.

- Seminars. K&A sponsors seminars within their areas of expertise. The firm's customers and prospective customers attend.

- Research. In one recent study, K&A surveyed new product and service professionals who introduced nearly 11,000 new products and services during the past five years. Among the findings: Ninety-four percent of successful companies said top management at their organization is committed to new product and service development. The research is sent to the media and presented at seminars.

"When you look at those seven components, all of which are activated simultaneously, there's a pretty good web to cast and reach prospects," says Kuczmarski. Suzanne Lowe, K&A's marketing director, coordinates the integrated effort.

Striking the Right Price

K&A's pricing strategy is based on a fixed-base fee. "We explain to clients what we will do for them and how long it will take. We tell them the price we will charge them and add that we have a history of being on budget. We don't try to sell a client one element and go back to them later and charge them more by telling them they will need some additional elements because the scope of the project has changed."

Priced less than the fees charged by such larger rivals as McKinsey and Booz Allen, K&A has eschewed billing on an hourly basis like many law and accounting firms because it builds distrust with the client, says Kuczmarski. "One of our key points of differentiation is how closely we work with our clients. We don't want anything to interfere with that."

"If you go to Andersen Consulting, a client will get a breakdown of different peoples' billing rates and their hours. You then multiply the rates by the hours," says Terrill. "We don't do it that way. We explain that our team of experts will deliver this type of result and here's the price. It's not: 'Here's the price of the bodies that are going to be involved in the project.'"

Tailoring the Work

The nature of the consulting work that K&A performs for its clients can take many forms. American Express, for example, hired K&A to do some idea generation for its Gold Card.

Rather than brainstorm, K&A went out and talked to business customers about what they did and didn't like. Besides lost luggage, the business travelers expressed frustration over not being able to accumulate all the air mile credits for travel on many different airlines without having to belong to every program.

K&A recommended that business travellers be awarded air mile credits from flying with a variety of airlines. The Membership Miles program became a success for American Express.

A Wide Range of Clients

K&A's clients range from such Fortune 500 companies as IBM Corporation, 3M Company and Rubbermaid, Inc., to small service companies with annual revenues of $50 million. "Our target market is businesses that have new products and services, and marketing strategy problems," says Kuczmarski.

Although K&A lacks the network of global offices of a McKinsey or a Booz Allen, Kuczmarski says a majority of U.S. businesses would consider a small consultancy. "I'd say about a third of the market is brand conscious. They want the security and safety of a big firm." But he says it doesn't make sense for potential clients to rule out K&A for projects because it has only 30 people versus 2,500 at McKinsey.

"Both of us will submit proposals in which a team of six or seven people will do the work. Whether it's six out of the 30 people at Kuczmarski or six out of 2,500 people at McKinsey, the fact is you'll still end up with six people." And if the work falls within one of the firm's specialties, Kuczmarski argues that K&A's work will be superior.

In other words, K&A is an underdog only in terms of its size, not by the quality of its work.

Cultivating a Unique Culture

An important reason that Kuczmarski believes the firm's handiwork is better than that turned out by the mega-consultancies, is K&A's culture. "Morale has an enormous impact on a professional's productivity and resulting impact on the quality of his or her work for a client."

The larger firms with their pyramidal hierarchies and complex politics can find it more difficult to produce high-quality consulting work. Internal problems can weigh on the quality of the external work, he maintains.

"We've tried to build a culture where people feel good about working here and more importantly, good about themselves. We use a rectangular, rather than a pyramidal model that allows everyone, including the senior people, to get deep into projects and hone their expertise.

"You grow at the big firms by selling. Senior partners at McKinsey spend 30 percent of their time consulting and 70 percent selling and networking. Here, you grow by becoming an expert. It's a much different career path, but one that differentiates us from our competitors."

PEOPLES BANK

When the three biggest banks in Indianapolis were snapped up by large, out-of-state institutions, William E. "Mac" McWhirter, president of Peoples Bank Corp., saw the opportunity of a lifetime.

Seizing on the backlash against the big dogs from Ohio and Michigan, Peoples reminded people in America's 12th-largest city that it has been locally-owned since 1891 and planned to stay that way.

"Our commercial loan officers were hearing from companies daily that were disenchanted over the impact of out-of-state control of the banks they had been doing business with," says McWhirter, whose great-grandfather, Felix T. McWhirter, founded the bank. "We saw Indianapolis as one of the best markets in the U.S. to be operating a bank and we'd been operating ours for more than 100 years."

Banking on the hunch that local ownership was a distinct, competitive advantage, Peoples Bank aggressively positioned itself as the hometown stalwart that truly knew what consumers and small- to mid-sized business wanted from a bank.

A sign in the lobby of Peoples' main office listed the Indianapolis banks that had been purchased by out-of-state bank holding companies. The sign pointed out that Peoples was not on the list.

In short, Peoples took several key steps to outmarket the competition. It:

- reinforced its position as a local bank with local interests;
- hired new loan officers to take advantage of a "once-in-a-lifetime opportunity;"
- conducted an intensive round of mail, phone and nose-to-nose customer surveys to determine exactly what they wanted in a period of rapid change in the local banking industry;
- focused intently on the small- to medium-sized business segment; and
- relied on "pluck, not luck."

Competitors Swoop In

Peoples, with about $400 million in assets, could hardly go nose-to-nose with Columbus, Ohio-based Banc One and its more than $75 billion in assets. Banc One, a super-regional bank, was the first out-of-state banking giant to swoop into Indiana with the 1986 purchase of American Fletcher National Bank.

In 1992, Cleveland-based National City Corporation acquired Merchants National and NBD Bancorp of Detroit bought INB Financial Corporation. Both Merchants and INB were well-established Indianapolis institutions, as were their legendary advertising mascots, the INB buffalo and the Merchants frog.

Peoples Bank noted the demise of those banks' independence in a series of award-winning ads that tweaked the mascots' departure.

The headline on an advertisement featuring the Merchants frog waving good-bye stated: "It won't be the same without him. (It *really* won't be the same.)" The text stated: "But if you bank at Peoples, you'll never have to say good-bye to local ownership. Peoples is *the* Indianapolis bank."

In another ad, the headline asks: "Where do you go when the buffalo roam?" The reference was to INB's trademark buffalo which appeared in the ad, heading off the corner of the page toward Detroit.

Differentiating Through Service

To reinforce its long record of customer service and innovation, an all-type ad stated: "The first Indianapolis bank to offer Saturday hours. ...The first Indianapolis bank to install drive-up windows. ...The first Indianapolis bank to grant an FHA loan. ...The first Indianapolis bank to elect a woman to the Board of Directors. ...Not bad for the last Indianapolis bank."

Although Peoples Bank wanted to show its frisky, underdog nature, there was the risk that the campaign could inflame the newly arrived banking giants, says Craig Stilwell, the bank's senior vice president of marketing.

"I thought there might be a small risk before I showed the ad campaign to Mac," says Stilwell. "We agreed that the big banks usually don't respond to our marketing. We're not a big enough threat to them. They're at least 20 times our size. We're after only a small percentage of the same business."

Big Banks Hold Their Fire

McWhirter was right. The big banks did not retaliate in their advertising nor did they target Peoples' customer base with a round of discounted loans or special offers.

In fact, a top executive of one of the banks which had been acquired wrote to say that he thought the campaign was well done. "It's not so much what you say in an ad, but how you say it. The campaign showed some genuine affection for the mascots. That's why I don't think it offended anyone."

Although not reacting directly to the Peoples print and broadcast campaign, Otto N. Frenzel, chairman of the former Merchants National Bank and now chairman of National City Bank, told the *Indianapolis Star* that the loss of local ownership was not a genuine concern.

"We will still be an Indiana bank with a thrust from Indianapolis to service the credit needs of our customer base here," Frenzel told the newspaper.

"It was Mr. Frenzel who said that, not his customers," says Stilwell. "We conducted focus groups and surveys which told us that local ownership did make a difference."

Adds McWhirter: "Mr. Frenzel is correct that some people don't care about local ownership. We have only about 5 percent of the local banking market. But let's say that 15 percent of the people in the market would prefer working with a bank that is locally-owned, but 85 percent do not.

"That 15 percent would be more business than we could ever handle. That 15 percent is a huge niche that do care and our research indicates there is a service-sensitive element out there and that's who the campaign was intended to reach." Peoples is proud of the fact that it closes a very high proportion of loans that it approves—about 80 percent.

Losing Its Distinction

Ironically, Peoples' distinction as the only locally-owned bank in Indianapolis was short-lived. Prompted by the loss of bank head-quarters in Indianapolis, a group of local businessmen launched the National Bank of Indianapolis in 1993.

Peoples, which could no longer call itself the only locally-owned bank, then declared itself the *oldest* locally-owned bank. Peoples didn't seem too bent out of shape by the launch of National Bank. In fact, it used the creation of a fellow banking underdog as the basis of a print ad whose headline read:

"After all the out-of-state takeovers, we'd like to welcome the new local bank. Maybe this Indianapolis thing is catching on." The text stated: "It's refreshing to see more local ownership, so here's to the new kid on the block." Atop the page was an illustration of a business publication heralding the arrival of National Bank of Indianapolis.

Amassing the Assets

The Midwestern regional banking powers that began staking turf in Indiana after it passed a multi-state banking law in 1985 have more than 80 percent of the $13 billion in deposits in all Indianapolis financial institutions. Indiana had become a sort of colony for the big, out-of-state banks, and some Hoosiers resented that colonial status.

That's why Peoples couldn't afford to pass up the opportunity to launch a print and broadcast campaign touting its hometown advantage. Peoples, which Stilwell says does its best marketing through face-to-face selling and word-of-mouth referrals from key customers, invested in its biggest advertising campaign ever. "Media is expensive and mass media is very expensive, so we tend not to do very much television," says Stilwell.

Although the new banks apparently came in peace, McWhirter and Stilwell were still eager to exploit that sense of disenchantment they detected in the local business community.

Creating a War Chest

Peoples sold a chunk of its non-voting stock through an initial public offering, raising $10 million to help the bank expand during that window of opportunity. The bank used the money to hire new sales representatives, credit analysts and commercial loan officers.

Peoples opened a new mortgage production office on the city's south side and restructured its branch system. "We're not sitting back and letting the business come to us," says McWhirter. "We initiated calling quotas and sales quotas that we never had in the past. We're out selling aggressively.

"Being locally owned and managed is one of the reasons we get to meet a lot of our new prospects. They are people we would not have been able to meet otherwise."

Peoples, which divides its revenues almost evenly between retail and commercial customers, will consider acquiring other local banks if the conditions are right, such as the right price or if the target bank has a similar operating philosophy, says McWhirter. "We would only be interested in growing in concentric circles. We would not acquire a bank outside the market area."

Carving out a Niche

While the city's Big Three banks can make loans in the $50 million to $100 million range, McWhirter says he gets nervous when Peoples cuts a loan for more than $1 million. "We have the capability of lending between $3 million and $5 million, but we rarely go above $3 million, which we have established as our in-house limit."

A conservative bank, Peoples' loan portfolio represents about 60 percent of its assets. Aggressive banks will lend up to 90 percent of their assets. Because of its self-imposed, as well as regulatory, limits on how much it can loan, Peoples' target commercial market is companies with sales ranging from $1 million to $20 million. The small- to mid-sized company niche is competitive and becoming more so as the big banks begin eyeing this fast-growing segment. The reasons for this are two-fold.

First, more big companies are turning to Wall Street rather than the big banks for their financial needs. Second, employment growth at the big companies has been virtually non-existent in this era of corporate downsizing.

"The real employment growth is taking place among the smaller companies," says McWhirter.

Encountering New Competitors

"We've recognized that, in the last few years, the big banks are targeting that market. We're running into the big banks more often than we used to. A few years ago, we'd never bump into them."

The bigger banks in Indianapolis have been advertising to the small- to mid-sized company. "But when you hear things like '20,000 people who care,' you know it's a just a slogan. I hope the small-business owner does, too," says Stilwell, whose bank employs 250 people.

Peoples can argue convincingly that its small-business customers will get more tender loving care than they would from its out-of-state-based competitors. "We don't even have a loan committee," says Stilwell. "Our account managers have the authority to grant credit. That decision doesn't have to go through a bureaucracy or be determined out of state."

Cultivating a Long-Term Relationship

"Often, the account manager who opens the account for a commercial customer will continue to serve that customer and be around to write that company's fourth or fifth loan. It's a close, long-term relationship," says McWhirter.

"At the big banks, the small-business market is typically a training ground for those who want to become commercial lenders in the larger market. If they're successful, they will grow their loan portfolio in a hurry into larger businesses. Because the turnover is so much higher, a customer will not work very long with that account person."

Active in the local business community, McWhirter says he's heard some executives from the city's Big Three banks express frustration over having to get matters approved in Detroit, Columbus or Cleveland. "I'm talking about some people fairly high up in their organizations. Imagine how their customers feel."

Pluck, Not Luck

Underscoring the theme of local ownership and personal service has helped fuel Peoples' double-digit growth rates of the past several years. The bank's motto once was "Not luck, but pluck." The phrase was coined by McWhirter's grandfather, Felix M., who guided the bank through the hard times of the Depression.

McWhirter realizes Peoples will need all the pluck and luck it can muster to continue prospering in the shadow of the Midwestern banking giants. He knows that the bank will not win by trying to compete on price. Small banks usually aren't the low-cost producers.

"We won't try to be everything to everybody. We'll focus on the kinds of customers we know we can please and stick with what we are good at. People still care to bank where they are well-known and can be important customers.

"This may sound like an odd comparison to make, but the difference between Peoples and a big bank is like the difference between a family-owned hardware store and a big chain operation. Walk into a family-owned operation, and even if the owner isn't there, the staff will make you feel like you belong there. It's a tangible feeling for a customer."

TATTERED COVER

When the Tattered Cover Book Store moved to larger digs in Denver, the store's customers volunteered to help lug boxloads of books that would line the shelves in a converted four-story department store.

To say the least, the Tattered Cover has a loyal following. How many companies can get their customers to sign up for grunt work? Owner Joyce Meskis has earned her customers' loyalty by simply making them feel at home.

"They have an emotional bond with the store because we treat them on a one-to-one basis," says Meskis, who aims to make her bookstore as comfortable and familiar as a living room or book-lined study. "Some customers need and appreciate lots of assistance, others would prefer to be left alone to page through a book. We have a very diverse population of readers and we do everything we can to keep them happy."

It's easy to understand why customers feel so welcome at the Tattered Cover. In the childrens' section there are rocking chairs. In the religious books sections, church pews.

Customers need not show identification when writing a check for a book purchase, no matter how large. Her 365-member work force of college students and bibliophiles, whom she calls "lifers," are scrupulously trained to never make judgmental remarks about the reading tastes of customers, who can choose from a vast array of books on everything from architecture to zoology. A new employee's first day of training includes a customer service seminar taught by Meskis, one of the true masters of the craft.

If a customer wants a book—any book in any language—the Tattered Cover will get it for them. The Tattered Cover special orders more than 400 books a day for customers from all over the world. The store has a reputation for its dogged pursuit of out-of-print books requested by customers. It's been said that if the Tattered Cover doesn't have a book or can't track it down, the book probably doesn't exist.

Large, overstuffed sofas and chairs and reading lamps through-out her store in Denver's Cherry Creek North neighborhood add to the homey touch that the chain bookstores sprouting up around her store and throughout Denver find hard to replicate.

It's no wonder that best-selling business author Tom Peters describes the Tattered Cover as "arguably the best bookstore in America."

"We have, over the years, established a pretty solid reputation with the community in terms of offering service, a broad selection and a pleasant place in which to do business. That's our stock in trade," says Meskis, who attributes the store's success to book-loving employees who are as devoted as the customers. The Tattered Cover also sells stationery, calendars, greeting cards and magazines.

Surviving a Darwinian Struggle

The Cherry Creek area is chock full of bookstores.

A 40,000-square-foot Barnes & Noble superstore has a store near the Tattered Cover and has established four other stores through-out Denver and neighboring Boulder. Also peddling books in Cher-ry Creek are chains such as Waldenbooks and Brentano's.

The plot in the Darwinian battle for survival among Denver booksellers thickened in the spring of 1994 when MusicLand opened four new Mediaplay stores. The 50,000-square-foot super-stores carry a mix of music, videos and books.

The first casualty in the struggle for book buyers was a Double-day bookstore. For the Tattered Cover, its high degree of intimacy became an important point of differentiation that continues to serve as the basis of its marketing strategy.

Retail Square Footage Rises Sharply

"In a two-year period, we have seen the square footage of retail booksellers increase dramatically. That has had an enormous impact on the community at large," says Meskis.

When asked if there's room for everyone, Meskis says: "We'll see. It's difficult to know what kind of fallout there might be from all the new competition. Some of the chains are already repositioning themselves."

But she's hardly running scared. Nor is she considering selling her store to a chain operation.

In the fall of 1994, the Tattered Cover opened its second store. Located in the restored and historically protected warehouse district in downtown Denver known as "LoDo," the new store is warmly appointed with wood floors and beams. "The nearly 100-year-old building has a warm and inviting feel," says Meskis, a former president of the American Booksellers Association.

A Big-Store Pioneer

Ironically, Meskis, who's working hard to differentiate her store from the big chain operations on the strength of the store's legendary customer service, is widely credited with creating the bookstore superstore when she moved the Tattered Cover into a converted, four-story department store in 1986. With 50,000 square feet of space, the bookstore boasts up to 225,000 titles in stock at any one time, and more than 600,000 books displayed on the shelves.

The Tattered Cover's competitive struggle is not unique. Independent bookstores are dwindling in the face of intensifying chain-store competition. More than 50 independents have closed their main stores or branches since late 1993, according to the American Booksellers Association. The independents' share of unit book sales dropped to 19 percent in 1994 from 32.5 percent in 1991.

Yet, Tattered Cover stores are prospering. And although the personal touch is the Tattered Cover bookstore's forte, Meskis takes a number of other marketing initiatives into consideration to keep the books selling. They include:

■ **Hosting special events.** The Tattered Cover sponsors more than 250 events a year, from folk dancing to women's groups meetings. There are weekly poetry readings and, every year, there's the Tattered Cover Halloween story contest.

■ **Book signings by authors.** The Tattered Cover has as many as 20 a month, with authors ranging from mystery writer Dick Francis to famed photographer Annie Leibovitz.

■ **Seminars.** To appeal to the businesspeople working near the new downtown store, the Tattered Cover sponsors what it calls its "Business Books and Brown Bag Lunch" program. Held during lunchtime or immediately after work, the program features business authors who talk about their books and share advice.

The Tattered Cover, which has a 2,000-square-foot special events room that can accommodate up to 200 people at its downtown store, inaugurated a travel seminar series in 1995. "The first program was on Scandinavia and the second was on Mexico. They have been 'wall busters,'" says Meskis.

■ **Catering to conventions or business conferences.** The store has a special department to work with meeting planners and outside groups holding meetings in Denver. "We can help provide attendees at a convention special reading materials that coincide with their areas of interest."

■ **Specialty newsletters.** In addition to publishing the "Tattered Cover" newsletter twice a year, the store's marketing department produces specialty newsletters for audiences such as children or businesspeople. The newsletters are mailed to customers in the store's vast database of 110,00 names worldwide. The publications can also be picked up in the store.

■ **Internet access.** With a presence on the Internet, the global computer network, customers armed with a credit card can order any book in the Tattered Cover stock. Special orders can also be transacted via the Internet. Electronic, worldwide access is important because Tattered Cover's legion of customers is spread throughout the world, Meskis notes.

"Because Denver is a big business center, people end up being transferred all over the world. The Internet allows them to stay in touch with us," says Meskis, who notes business over the Internet is a small, but growing, portion of her company's business.

■ **Print advertising.** The Tattered Cover, says Meskis, can't match the advertising expenditures of her chain competitors, which frequently take out full-page ads in the local newspapers. Ads for the Tattered Cover appear throughout the year in the *Rocky Mountain News, Denver Post* and *Westward,* a weekly entertainment publication. Ads also appear in neighborhood publications around Denver.

Avoiding a Price War

The Tattered Cover has not been drawn into the price war that has been the ruin of so many independent bookstores. "Certainly discounting has been MediaPlay's and Barnes & Nobles' stock in trade," says Meskis.

"We do not discount. We have the occasional sale and we have a huge selection of bargain books. While we have offered a sampling of bargain books from the beginning, we began offering a substantial selection back in 1983. It's something our customers find of value." At the Tattered Cover, customers can find the $1 book. At the other end of the price spectrum, a customer can spend more than $2,000 for a multi-volume set of the Oxford English Dictionary.

With an eye toward the competition, the Tattered Cover pushed back its closing time from 9 p.m. to 11 p.m. and added coffee to the mix at both stores. Meskis also continues to raise book awareness outside the walls of the store. She lectures frequently to civic groups, and programs are crafted and presented for specialty groups by the managers and store buyers.

The Tattered Cover will differentiate itself on service, not price, Meskis reiterates.

Turning Over a New Leaf

In the spring of 1995, the Tattered Cover added food to its menu of offerings with the opening of "The Fourth Story." The 100-seat, full-service restaurant features fresh, wholesome American cuisine and, as the name suggests, is on the fourth floor of the Cherry Creek store.

"Like the store itself, we created an inviting, browsing atmosphere. With Pike's Peak in the distance, the views are quite spectacular. The restaurant is a way for us to reaffirm our unique position in the Denver market. Frankly, the restaurant is something we would have done regardless of all the new competition. There had been a restaurant in that space up until about 1988."

The new restaurant, like her two bookstores, were designed by Meskis, who allows that a professional designer handled the kitchen's layout. The restaurant, graced with shelves full of books, employs about 40 people working specifically for Tattered Cover Food and Beverage Inc., a unit of Tattered Cover Inc.

Suffering an Initial Setback

The creation of the nation's largest and most admired independent bookstores began in 1974 when Meskis purchased the Tattered Cover, a 950-square-foot store that had been launched three years earlier.

Her first stab at bookselling had ended in failure. She had bought a small bookstore in Parker, Colorado, about 20 miles southeast of Denver. It was a planned community with robust growth plans. When the growth didn't materialize, Meskis' tiny bookstore venture went up in smoke.

She didn't brood about the failure. Instead, she went out and borrowed money from every willing acquaintance, friend or family member to buy the Tattered Cover. The money has long since been repaid.

Planning to Be a Professor

A native of Chicago's rough-and-tumble South Side, Meskis originally planned to be math professor. To help defray her tuition at Purdue University, she began working at bookstores and the university library.

She continued to work in libraries and bookstores while in graduate school at the University of Denver. Influenced by her love of books, Meskis switched her academic interest to English. Although she never became an English professor, she's been surrounded by books ever since.

A champion of free expression, Meskis received the PEN/ Newman's Own First Amendment Award during ceremonies in New York in the spring of 1995. Judges included playwright Tony Kushner and novelist Alice Hoffman.

Meskis' qualifications for the award include her refusal to discontinue selling Salman Rushdie's book "The Satanic Verses." She donated 25 percent of the proceeds from the sale of the Rushdie book to anti-censorship groups. In 1994, she formed Colorado Citizens Against Censorship to fight a proposed amendment to the Colorado constitution that would have given communities broad powers in declaring materials "obscene."

A Test of Mettle

She has every confidence that the Tattered Cover bookstores, despite the growing competition from the chains, will continue to flourish.

"I'm an eternal optimist and firmly believe there is a place in this world for independent bookstores. I've been through some difficult challenges over the course of 22 years in bookselling and the current situation is a particularly challenging one.

"This will test the mettle of all of us here at the Tattered Cover. We are not letting the grass grow under our feet—especially now."

She offers a simple formula for the success of independent bookstores facing larger competitors: "Cultivate and maintain your own, unique personality. That's a bookstore's greatest strength."

EDWARD D. JONES & CO.

Brokerage firm Edward D. Jones & Co. says you can have Wall Street. They'll take Main Street.

The St. Louis-based brokerage has traditionally hung out its shingle on the Main Streets in small towns across America. Unlike the big Wall Street-based investment houses such as Merrill Lynch and Paine Webber which operate offices in big cities around the country staffed with scores of brokers, Jones assigns only one broker per office.

If it sounds like an existence as lonely as the Maytag repairman's, it's not. Each day, Jones' brokers press the flesh of dozens of people in the community. It's that brand of face-to-face, one-on-one marketing and selling that the Wall Streeters can't possibly match. It is the firm's primary differentiator.

One Office, One Broker

Assigning one broker per office makes for a lot of offices. In fact, if brokerage firms were measured by their number of branch offices, Jones would be the biggest in the business. It has more than 3,300 retail offices in such places as Thief River Falls, Minnesota; Cut Bank, Montana; and Broken Bow, Nebraska.

While conservative investors in small towns remain its core customers, Jones has been breaking out of its long-held rural niche in the past 10 years by expanding aggressively into the suburbs of such big cities as Chicago, Atlanta, Los Angeles and Toronto.

About 60 percent of its customers hail from small towns, 40 percent from metropolitan areas. In the Chicago area alone, Jones plans to open 275 retail offices. Regardless of where Jones plants its flag, the one-to-one selling philosophy prevails, explains John W. Bachmann, managing principal of the firm founded in 1922.

Penetrating the Suburbs

Jones' bullish move into the suburban strongholds of the major Wall Street brokerages is not likely to incur the wrath of the big dogs, says Bachmann. "The big firms have never taken us all that seriously. And why should they? They take a much different

approach to the market. I don't think a firm like ours, whose investing philosophy is 'buy-and-hold,' represents any threat to them.

"In a sense, we compete nose-to-nose with the big firms, but we
are differentiating ourselves in the marketplace. If you look at our
offices, we look different. If you hear what we have to say, we sound
different. And if you look at what we have to sell, we are different.
The market is so big that we barely make a ripple," says Bachmann,
whose firm's revenues top $600 million, a far cry from Merrill
Lynch's $18 billion in annual revenues.

By the turn of the century, Jones projects it will have 10,000
retail offices. Maybe Wall Street *should* start worrying about keeping
up with the Joneses.

Avoiding Wall Street

The firm has a branch office in Queens and one in Brooklyn, but it
has no plans to open one on Wall Street. Jones plans to remain true
to its roots on Main Street where the hard-sell usually doesn't sell.

Jones is not only smaller, but more focused, contends Bachmann,
who's been at Jones' helm since 1980. Bachmann has overseen the
firm's rapid expansion, primarily into metropolitan areas, and a
broadening of the investment products it offers.

Despite rapid growth and a more diversified product line, Jones
retains its clear sense for who its 1.6 million customers are. Jones'
target audience consists of:
- Retirees
- People preparing to retire
- Small-businesspeople

It's the ranchers, farmers and the merchants in the nation's
smaller communities who welcome the one-on-one investment
information that would be almost impossible to get if Jones were
not in the small towns, says Bachmann. Typical Jones' customers,
regardless of where they live, are middle-aged to older men and
women looking for safe havens for their retirement nest eggs.

Playing to its Strength

Management guru Peter Drucker has long counseled Jones on its operational and marketing strategies. Drucker continues to advise Jones to concentrate on its strong suit, which he identified as a laser-like focus on a well-defined set of customers and an equally well-defined investment philosophy.

Making it easy to carry it all forward are the individual brokers, or "investment representatives," as they are known at Jones. "Our investment representatives are our profit centers. Our whole organization is designed around making that IR effective. The IR's don't compete against each other."

Driving Jones' marketing success are several factors:

■ **A strong belief in grassroots marketing.** A first-year broker is required to visit the homes or businesses of 1,200 prospective customers to introduce himself and explain the Jones investment philosophy.

The broker receives a small and diminishing salary during the first year. As the customer base grows, the broker's compensation converts to a commission, typically by the end of the first year. Jones pays for start-up expenses such as office furniture and supplies, and pays the salary of an administrative assistant.

Jones doesn't want its brokers working the phones, but working the streets in the community. "We go face-to-face and meet 20 or so people a day. It's a very personal business," says Bachmann, who spent seven years as a Jones rep in Columbia, Missouri, before being tapped for a larger corporate role.

"That Jones representative will go out and get involved in the local Chamber of Commerce and get involved in business organizations wherever he or she can meet people. Hopefully, they'll be asked to join the Rotary Club. We want them out and visible in the community.

"That way people can decide whether that person is somebody who really knows their stuff and would do the kind of conscientious job that our customers are looking for.

"At a brokerage like Charles Schwab, 99 percent of the business is done by phone. My guess is that 90 percent of the business conducted by the Wall Street firms is done by the phone. Ninety percent of the business at Jones is not done over the phone."

People in communities where Jones has recently opened its doors are often surprised that its investment representatives are so readily available. "Our IR's are prepared to come by your home at 8 p.m. and sit down for two hours to discuss, for example, how to invest a lump sum payout for retirement."

■ **Brokers manage a single portfolio of customers.** Jones brokers don't mine up the accounts and then turn them over to be managed from the headquarters unit in St. Louis. A Jones rep operates on a one-to-one basis with the investor throughout the course of the relationship. The arrangement ensures that Jones remains "customer-focused, rather than product-focused," according to Bachmann.

Managing the customer's portfolio is simplified because of Jones' low-risk investment philosophy. Investment products offered by Jones include certificates of deposit, IRA's, mutual funds, annuities and common stock, although Jones does not sell stocks priced lower than $4 per share because it considers them too risky.

"We don't sell agricultural or financial futures or options on futures or securities," says Bachmann. "We don't encourage margin accounts. You can have one, but we encourage customers to use their accounts for borrowing, not to buy securities."

■ **Hiring and training the right people.** Because it endows each rep with so much authority and responsibility, Jones works hard to find the right person. "We want people who have a burning desire to be in the investment business," says Bachmann. "They must be comfortable with building long-term relationships and selling face-to-face."

Jones isn't looking for MBA's. "We take people from all walks of life—teachers, police officers, engineers, even bank presidents. Because they're so comfortable talking to people about their money, bankers have been very successful with us. The key ingredients are the background and the aptitude.

"We attract people who are high achievers and who value the freedom that comes with managing their own offices and, in many ways, their own business," says Bachmann. In other words, people lacking an entrepreneurial spirit need not apply.

When staffing its new retail offices in Dallas several years ago, Bachmann says Jones made the serious mistake of hiring too many people whose hearts weren't in the business. "For people just looking for a job, this kind of work is just too hard."

Many of the Dallas hires were recruited at job fairs, but weren't committed to the investment business, as Jones painfully discovered. "As soon as a better job came along, they quit. We spent a lot of money and had nothing to show for it."

Bachmann proudly recalls the story of a Jones rep in Montana who drove five hours each way to spend a day helping out a struggling young colleague. "The older fellow didn't want any credit or special attention for what he did on his own time. I didn't hear about it for years. But it's people like that that this firm is made of."

New hires are extensively trained at Jones headquarters. Once in the field, the reps continue to be trained via a satellite system that links each of the 3,300 branches with headquarters. The system, which provides both voice and video programming, is frequently used for in-service sales training and seminars on the firm's product mix.

One of the firm's most effective training methods is a mentoring system in which a more experienced investment representative spends a day or two with a novice colleague to share advice. The trainer is not compensated. "Their only reward is a sense that they're giving something back. That can only be done in a system where everybody is pulling in the same direction," says Bachmann.

An industry publication, *Registered Representative,* recognized Jones for scoring the highest in 18 of 19 categories used to rate brokerages in its December 1994 issue. Major categories evaluated were work environment, support, product and management.

The publication's results were based on telephone surveys of employees of the nation's nine largest brokerage firms. One Jones respondent said even though Jones was a large, national operation, it still had a "smallish feel" that brokers enjoy. Another noted that teamwork rather than competition was the watchword at Jones.

■ **Savvy use of technology.** In 1990, Jones launched the largest private satellite network in the financial services industry. Jones clients can place orders and, within 20 seconds, know the price paid, including the commission.

One of the firm's featured systems is MarketScope, a computer service provided by Standard & Poor's Corporation. MarketScope can instantly produce information on 5,000 companies. The service also provides buy, sell and hold recommendations on more than 1,000 companies.

Using a teletype-based communications system through the late 1970's seriously limited the company's ability to communicate both internally and externally. "When we began hiring more investment representatives, offering more products and expanding into new markets, the system went into gridlock. We had to stop our growth in 1978."

Development of a modern telecommunications system began in the early 1980's and was a major catalyst for firm's rapid growth. Using a system that would seem primitive by today's standards "allowed us to finally communicate on a split-second basis. We were able to handle a lot more information."

■ **Limited use of mass media advertising.** Because its 3,300 investment representatives work the streets to personally deliver Jones' marketing messages, the firm uses a relatively small amount of advertising.

"We've not figured out how to run national advertising," admits Bachmann. "TV is much too expensive. We do run a piece on page 2 of *The Wall Street Journal* every two weeks, which is really more of a philosophical statement on investment-related matters. We have talked about global investing or spelled out investment strategies."

Because of the grassroots nature of its business, Jones advertises in local and community newspapers. The ads typically feature the local investment representative.

Small-Town Opportunities

It's the local IR that has been the backbone of the company, particularly since 1955 when Edward "Ted" Jones Jr., son of the founder, recognized that small towns were largely ignored by the investment industry. "Ted recognized that people in rural America needed advice on buying quality investments, too," says Bachmann.

Despite his father's belief that the firm should open branches in larger cities, the younger Jones opened the firm's first branch office in Mexico, Missouri. In 1955, the town's population was about 12,000. From the small Missouri town, Jones "rode the circuit" visiting small towns throughout the Midwest and down south to Louisiana.

"It woke Ted up to the fact that he didn't have to travel a circuit. A community as small as 10,000 could support an investment representative." Jones then brought Wall Street to dozens of small communities and connected them to St. Louis via the teletype.

By the 1960's, Jones had established a network of about 90 offices. The firm began to stall as the stock market went sour in the late 1960's. Bachmann moved to headquarters in 1970 where he was charged with the task of developing other investment products.

Broadening the Product Line

Bachmann broadened the product line to include tax-exempt bonds, annuities, taxable government and corporate bonds, and over-the-counter stocks. "Prior to that, a customer would come to one of the offices and ask about different investment vehicles. When all you had to sell was stocks, you wouldn't get very far."

By 1980, after Ted Jones' death, the firm came to recognize that its market wasn't geographically distinct, and thus began the technology-driven expansion into new communities and large metropolitan areas.

Appreciating the Historic

Even though many suburbs are nothing more than endless vistas of housing tracts and strip malls, some do have downtowns with character. Jones representatives like to set up shop in the heart of business districts and often in restored buildings. In the Chicago suburb of Palatine, for example, the Jones representative's office is in a former fire station.

In Duluth, Minnesota, the Jones representative occupies an office in a theater built in 1926. The Jones broker in Milford, Connecticut, does business from a former newspaper office built in 1799. Jones is so committed to maintaining the vitality of Main Streets in both suburbs and rural communities that it teamed up with the National Main Street Center of the National Trust.

Using its state-of-the-art teleconferencing system in St. Louis, Jones has transmitted satellite broadcasts on the subject of revitalized downtown business districts to its branch offices. Jones representatives with an interest in the subject invite their small-business clients to watch or participate by calling Main Street officials on a toll-free line.

Jones and Main Street jointly produced a videotape to help promote a downtown revitalization project.

Keeping the Original Focus

As Jones continues marching toward its goal of opening 10,000 branch offices, Bachmann assures that the company will never lose sight of its one-to-one customer focus that plays so well on Main Street.

"The biggest argument among the partners, not long after I became one, was the belief that we'd cease to become one big happy family if we ever had more than 100 offices. My guess is that we're a lot closer to that big, happy family feeling with 3,300 offices than we were then. I think that's because we've designed a system based on cooperation rather than competition, which then lets us focus on our customer."

EXECUTIVE FEMALE

Advertisers looking for targeted media vehicles to reach the growing number of women in the work force have a wealth of magazines to choose from: *Working Woman, Executive Female, Female Entrepreneur, Working Mother* and others.

While each title caters to its own unique niche within the female work force, those magazines that offer advertisers the most well-defined readership and the most opportunities to add value to their messages will continue to grow, says Brenda S. Ginsberg, marketing director for *Executive Female* magazine.

"We want to establish a relationship with our advertisers so they see us as a kind of mini-marketing department that develops opportunities for them to more effectively get the word out on their products and services," says Ginsberg.

Building Bonds With Advertisers

Unlike some publishers who are content to take an advertiser's money in exchange for a page or two in the magazine, Ginsberg says *Executive Female* has to go beyond the "take the money and run" philosophy.

"We've developed a close relationship with our advertisers. I'm on the phone all the time with them." And it's not just to sell pages in the magazine, but to develop programs and events that will allow advertisers to strike a closer relationship with *Executive Female*'s readers.

Published by the National Association for Female Executives (NAFE), the bi-monthly publication is a membership perk for the organization's nearly 250,000 members. New York-based NAFE has about 225 chapters in the U.S. as well as chapters in Japan, Canada and Israel.

Because the publication is mailed only to NAFE members, *Executive Female* doesn't have to slug it out on the newstands like consumer or large business-oriented magazines that scrap for circulation gains.

Differentiating Through Focus

The battle for advertisers—the folks who pay the bulk of the freight at magazines—can be just as intense, however, says Ginsberg, who must often argue her case against advertisers considering *Working Woman*, the largest publication in the field.

"We're the underdog in that situation," says Ginsberg, noting *Working Woman*'s 765,000 circulation is nearly three times that of *Executive Female*'s. "Our relationship with *Working Woman* is competitive, but not hostile. I'd say we are more focused than they are, but that's not to say that what they are doing isn't just as valuable to their reader as what we're doing for our reader."

To counter *Working Woman*'s greater clout in the marketplace, which includes a cable television program, "we have to be more creative and entrepreneurial," says Ginsberg, the former director of the American Women's Economic Development Corporation's National Conference.

A Powerful Reader Profile

Executive Female differentiates itself on the basis of its readership profile. "There's an almost pure demographic profile of our members in a sense. It's a cleaner audience," says Ginsberg, referring to the readership's concentration of executives ranging from middle management to the CEO. About 15 percent of the reader/members are entrepreneurs.

Working Woman cuts a broader swath through the work force, ranging from the clerical ranks to the boardroom.

"Although we have a much smaller circulation, we tell advertisers that they can buy a much 'cleaner' audience for less money. The advertiser has to decide what makes more sense."

Ginsberg, of course, will maintain that a page or year-long schedule of pages in *Executive Female* makes the most sense. She bases her marketing argument on several factors.

■ **An appealing demographic readership profile.** *Executive Female* can offer an advertiser more bang for its buck by virtue of its influential readership concentrated in the managerial ranks.

According to a readership study conducted for the magazine by the Gallup Organization:

- *Executive Female* readers have an average household income of $67,320;
- 91 percent attended or graduated from college; 24 percent have postgraduate degrees;
- 45 percent are married, 30 percent are single, 20 percent are divorced or separated and 3 percent are widowed;
- 62 percent own their own home or condominium; and
- 49 percent have investments and savings of more than $10,000.

The Gallup-commissioned profile of the readership's business characteristics indicated that:

- 60 percent held the titles of owner/partner, vice president, supervisor, director, manager or administrator;
- 37 percent had responsibility for 500 or more employees;
- 49 percent were responsible for budgets of more than $50,000; and
- a majority of the readers have decision-making authority for such products as offices supplies and equipment, computer hardware and software and the hiring of personnel.

"These are smart, influential women who pay attention to what's in the magazine," says Ginsberg. "Although women's income, on average, is only 75 percent of men's income, it is growing, and more advertisers are recognizing that."

To alert advertisers to the benefits of its powerful female audience, the magazine is beefing up its sales force and preparing to launch a direct mail campaign targeting major national advertisers, according to Ginsberg.

■ **Value-added programs for advertisers.** As an example of the partnership it strikes with an advertiser, *Executive Female* has worked closely with Edward D. Jones & Co., the brokerage firm discussed earlier in this chapter, to develop a four-part satellite conference series for professional women.

Using Jones' satellite-based telecommunications systems, the four, two-hour programs titled "Journey to Success" are beamed into Jones' branch offices around the country.

The conferences give the Jones representatives the opportunity to invite *Executive Female* readers to their offices. The sessions can often lead to the start of a customer relationship or renew an existing relationship.

The programs are offered in the evening to accommodate the professional woman's schedule. A $15 registration fee covers all broadcasts and the fee also renews NAFE membership for current members and serves as the membership fee for non-members.

The 1995 "Journey to Success" series featured presentations by Anita Roddick, founder of the Body Shop; Betsy Myers, an official with the Small Business Administration; and Gail Buckner, vice president of Putnam Mutual Funds.

The presentations were drawn from a series of satellite conferences that NAFE offers its general memberships and their guests. The $49 fee charged members includes a breakfast and a networking break. The programs have been sponsored by companies such as J.C. Penney and Lincoln-Mercury.

The Jones "Journey to Success" program arose from the relationship the brokerage firm developed as a regular advertiser in *Executive Female*. "We're both heavily into segment marketing, so we found each other," says Ginsberg.

Jones regularly runs an ad in the magazine featuring a female broker who shares her success story. The ad is designed to help recruit female brokers as well as promote its brokerage services. "The series has been successful for Jones. They've already trained several of our readers."

Using examples like Jones, Ginsberg says she can help sell prospective advertisers on the benefits of appearing in *Executive Female* through the use of case histories. "The results speak for themselves and that impresses an advertiser," she says.

Other major advertisers include Mutual of Omaha, Fidelity Investments, Janus Funds, Hertz, Avis, Bell Atlantic, the Betty Ford Center and H. Stern Jewelers. "With a number of advertisers, we offer programs in which readers get discounts if they use an advertiser's services, such as renting a car from Hertz or Avis," says Ginsberg.

Unlike independent publications, readers of an association publication have a greater affinity for not only the magazine itself but the advertisers as well, contends Ginsberg. A page of advertising in *Executive Female* is a bargain compared to *Working Woman*, which charges advertisers $38,500 to run a four-color ad on a one-time basis versus $6,976 for a four-color ad in *Executive Female*.

■ **Helping local advertisers access the professional women's market.** In the spring of 1995, *Executive Female* and the *St. Petersburg Times* jointly developed an advertising pullout section to run in that respected Florida daily.

The section mixes editorial from *Executive Female* and ads from marketers in the Tampa-St. Petersburg area. Several of *Executive Female*'s national advertisers expressed interest in the section as well.

"They're eager to participate at the local level," says Ginsberg, who adds that a one-day conference on issues important to women professionals would coincide with the release of the section. *Executive Female* is considering running similar sections in other major daily newspapers.

■ **An editorial focus on management issues and career advice.** Unlike *Working Woman*, whose editorial mix includes lifestyle articles to appeal to its broad audience and advertisers trying to reach that audience, *Executive Female* is strictly business.

"We keep our editorial pretty pure. That's not to say we won't add some lifestyle articles in the future, but our members look to us for advice on advancing their careers, networking, and 'how to' information from a manager's and entrepreneur's perspective."

Basia Hellwig, the publication's editor-in-chief, explained in her column in the March/April 1995 issue that one of the missions of *Executive Female* is to give its readers the tools to achieve career security.

"In every issue our aim is to give you insights, information and strategies that will help you craft a successful work life on your terms. Above all," Hellwig writes, "that means thinking of yourself not as an employee, but as a business. And it means taking personal responsibility for keeping that 'business' competitive and attuned to the marketplace."

In that same issue, Hellwig's staff presented stories such as the nuts and bolts of opening a coffee bar, tips on a "surprisingly simple way to make better decisions," what do about being stuck in a hated job, finding the right stockbroker, and how to fire up a staff with a powerful memo.

Executive Female, Ginsberg explains, differentiates itself from the general business magazines like *Fortune* and *Forbes* by using women exclusively as the role models. "We cover their success stories, as well as their failures to serve as lessons on how to avoid problems and turn things around."

4 The Reinventors

To differentiate a product or service in a competitive arena is smart marketing, but some companies go one better. They reinvent the market, in essence, making an end-run around the competition. The category in which a marketer operates may be old, but the tactics and strategies have a fresh new look, which often translates into a distinct competitive advantage. This may provide a quicker path to the top for an underdog marketer, though it is sometimes riskier.

Flowers, office products, beer and religion have been around a long time. But the one-time underdogs in this chapter have all taught the market a few new tricks through their dynamic marketing.

Jim McCann was running a single florist's shop in Manhattan in 1976. By 1995, he was running the world's largest florist, 1-800-FLOWERS. What McCann did was redefine how flowers can be bought, how quickly they're delivered, and how fresh they should be. His company's attentiveness to quality and customer service proved that a mass marketer could flourish in the floral industry.

Viking Office Products was just one of many small office supply and products mail-order houses in Los Angeles until Irwin Helford arrived. He changed the struggling company's fortunes by personalizing an impersonal sales channel.

It went beyond putting his picture on the company's catalogs. With a deft use of the company's sophisticated customer database, Viking mastered the art of micromarketing its product offerings to its growing base of worldwide small-business customers. Well on its way to $1 billion in sales, Viking has ensured its success in a reinvented sales channel by being "fanatical" about customer service.

Nor'Wester Brewery and Public House added a new twist to marketing beer by turning the new company's 8,000 shareholders loose on Portland with business cards and short messages delivered door-to-door. They must have sounded convincing, because Nor'Wester built a new brewhouse in 1995 to double production of its microbrewed Nor'Wester beer.

Even religion can be reinvented, as the Rev. H. Edwin Young and his Second Baptist Church have proved. The so-called "megachurch" reached out to its target audience of non-churchgoers in Houston through media blitzes, Disney-style special events and a non-intimidating brand of worship that has packed the pews of its 6,200-seat sanctuary. Second Baptist doesn't consider itself an underdog to pop culture.

Necessity proved to be the mother of reinvention for Christian Supply Centers, a Portland, Oregon, bookstore chain in a very mature stage of its life cycle. Under new ownership of Pamplin Publishing and the leadership of President Gary Randall, Christian Supply sprang back to life.

Randall introduced new lines of merchandise, a fresh look to the stores and and created a special-events-driven atmosphere that he says is a cross between "Barnes and Noble and the state fair."

Now, meet the Reinventors.

1-800-FLOWERS

Jim McCann never bought the argument that floral customers didn't need an 800 number, round-the-clock access, freshness guarantees, standard prices and an array of flowers always in inventory.

Had he believed that, Florist Transworld Delivery or FTD might still be the leading brandname in the $12 billion floral industry. Instead, 1-800-FLOWERS is.

McCann, a former social worker, reinvented the floral industry and now enjoys the spoils. Privately-held Westbury, New York-based 1-800-FLOWERS is now the world's largest florist with annual sales of a quarter of a billion dollars.

FTD Under Fire

About 23,000 of North America's 40,000 florists are members of FTD, a non-profit floral cooperative that has suffered from declining membership and sales in the past six years. The organization was criticized for responding too slowly to market changes. This was true, in part, because in order to make changes, FTD had had to seek consensus amongst far-flung members. In 1994, FTD was overhauled to make it more competitive.

FTD, McCann explains, acts as a trade group for its member florists and helps establish membership standards. Ironically, 1-800-FLOWERS is an FTD member—its largest single member. That explains why 1-800-FLOWERS doesn't position itself against FTD in its advertising. 1-800-FLOWERS uses the FTD electronic system to communicate orders to affiliated florists.

But McCann will state publicly that FTD wasn't aggressive enough at encouraging its members to "raise the bar" in terms of customer service. "For too long this industry got by with having shops open fewer than seven days a week and with hours that were less than comfortable for customers. Everyone was doing the same thing, so florists got away with it."

Flaunting Conventional Wisdom

"There were florists in the organization who told us that customers didn't want an 800 number, that they didn't want to be able to access us 24 hours a day, that they didn't want standardized pricing or freshness guarantees. They claimed that those things were unimportant to the customer. We felt differently and decided to press our agenda," says McCann.

"As time went by, FTD began to see that we were either the luckiest people in the world or that there was something to our message and our method. So very late in the game, FTD decided our success was more than just luck.

"They discovered that maybe the customer did want 24-hour access, convenience, better products and the value-added programs that we had brought to the table. In fairness, there were retail florists who weren't in lockstep with FTD, which purports to represent the universe of the membership. There are some very progressive retail florists in their own markets. But they were the exception rather than the rule."

1-800-FLOWERS took a number of key steps to reinvent the floral market. They include:

■ **Higher customer service standards.** 1-800-FLOWERS uses what it calls its 'est positioning' as in best, freshest, surest and fastest. "We are the 'est' provider of service in our category," says McCann.

"We are not the smartest, most creative people in the world, but shall we say we are the adaptors of good ideas and practices. We borrow ideas from other industries to benchmark our own performances."

1-800-FLOWERS borrows liberally from L.L. Bean, the legendary cataloger of rugged outdoor clothes and footwear. "L.L. Bean realized that if they were to lure department store shoppers, they would have to have the best service possible. That includes absolute guarantees, 24-hour service and products in inventory all the time."

The successful retailers of the '90s "can't just sit back and say they're going to be X. If your customer wants you to be Y and Z, you'd better be," says McCann.

■ **Freshness guarantees.** 1-800-FLOWERS initiated an industry-leading guarantee that any flowers you buy will stay fresh for one week. Flowers that wilt in seven days or fewer are replaced, no questions asked.

1-800-FLOWERS uses what it calls its Freshness Care System that begins by selecting the leading flower farms from around the world. As explained in "Fresh Thoughts," the company's newsletter, the flowers are cut as soon as they reach the proper stage.

Without wasting a moment, the flowers are hydrated, inspected and packed. Secured in protective boxes, the flowers are cooled to retard the aging process. Once the flowers arrive in retail stores, the stems are recut and placed in a hydrating solution. Once fully hydrated, flowers are placed in coolers in a mixture of floral nutrients.

■ **Adroit use of technology.** 1-800-FLOWERS has taken a leading role within the floral industry by making use of on-line shopping services, such as America Online, and providing customers with CD ROM catalogs and interactive television. The company has its own department totally dedicated to interactive services.

1-800-FLOWERS' marketing effort in cyberspace "is an opportunity for our people to work on something exciting and on the cutting edge. It makes us stand out and look different," says McCann. "It's great from a public relations standpoint and it's a good way to position for the future."

Although only about 10 percent of the company's orders are handled via on-line services or on the Internet, McCann says that percentage has been growing steadily. About 50 percent of sales come through the company's easy-to-remember phone number and 40 percent from 1-800-FLOWERS shops.

"We sell three different ways: 'telephonically,' electronically and good old-fashioned retail."

For the cyber shopper, 1-800-FLOWERS offers several interactive programs including:

- "Sure Winners." People unsure of what kind of flowers to give a friend, a business associate or a boss need only supply some information about the recipient. 1-800-FLOWERS suggests the appropriate arrangement.

- "Gift Registry." An entire year's worth of gift giving can be handled in one electronic session. Customers select the arrangements, give the dates and then sign off. 1-800-FLOWERS sends each gift on time with the right message.
- "Gift Reminders." This service is for people who never want to forget another anniversary or birthday. A customer is given 50 slots for special occasions. Five days before a special event, the customer receives an electronic message reminding them of the deadline.

1-800-FLOWERS' big splash in the interactive realm isn't designed to change its customers' buying habits.

"There's too much risk in doing that. What we're saying is that there are a variety of ways to buy flowers from us. Some of our customers have asked if they could buy on-line and we're giving them the opportunity. It opens up new channels for us. We don't put all our eggs in one basket."

Although telemarketing is hardly new, 1-800-FLOWERS recognized in the late 1980's that the technology has enormous potential to drive sales. "We rode the wave of opportunity created by telemarketing. You don't swim against a tide as strong as that," says McCann.

■ **Timely use of media.** The now-familiar 1-800-FLOWERS brand was given an enormous boost on CNN during the Persian Gulf War in 1991. 1-800-FLOWERS, which had been advertising since 1988 on the all-news cable channel owned by Ted Turner, did not pull its spots during the brief war.

"It was a very tense time and a lot of advertisers weren't sure what to do and cancelled their ads," says McCann. "We chose to keep running." It turned out to be a bonanza for 1-800-FLOWERS, which had bought air time on CNN before the war erupted.

When viewership increased more than twenty-fold, 1-800-FLOWERS gained a huge increase in recognition. 1-800-FLOWERS continues to build consumer awareness by spending more than $30 million a year on cable TV, radio, print, outdoor, direct mail and sales promotion. The company has also teamed up with AT&T and United Airlines for sales promotions.

■ **Capturing, and acting on, customer feedback.** "We have an in-house market research group that does nothing but talk to customers. They conduct tests of our products and services and index them as a way of measuring performance. Everyone's compensation is tied to those indexes.

"Before we go forward with a program, we ask the customers such questions as: 'What would make the product more attractive to you?;' 'What price points do you find attractive?;' or 'How can we make it more convenient for you?' All our new products are tailored so that they conform with what the customer wants."

To get a better sense of what kinds of flowers mothers want on Mother's Day, the market research group conducted a survey. Among the findings: moms prefer floral arrangements in a basket over a vase; bright colors are preferred over pastels; and a country garden style is preferred over a traditional arrangement.

Each year, 1-800-FLOWERS' "Mothers Who Matter Most" essay contest attracts more than 20,000 entries. Winners receive a trip anywhere in the U.S.

An Empire of Flowers

McCann's floral empire now extends to Oslo, Dublin and Mexico City, where it has struck partnerships with retail florists. Further international expansion is in the works.

It all started with a single florist shop in Manhattan that McCann bought in 1976 with his $10,000 life savings. Ten years later, he owned 14 flower shops around New York and was running a company that imported flowers from South America and Europe.

In 1987, McCann bought 1-800-FLOWERS, a foundering, three-year-old floral telemarketer based in Dallas. He moved operations to New York, where he kept a tight rein on costs, instituted the company's freshness guarantee and created a telemarketing center manned by 25 employees. Company revenues in those days were only about $400,000.

Expanding its Retail Base

By 1994, 1-800-FLOWERS had the financial wherewithal to buy Conroy's Flowers, the nation's largest flower chain, with more than 150 franchise operations in California and the Southwest. The name of the shops was changed from Conroy to 1-800-FLOWERS.

"People who knew me back in my social worker days ask how I became a florist. I tell them it really wasn't that much of a leap. Whether I was running a home for troubled boys or the world's largest florist, my job is to put individuals together and find in those individuals skills and talents that if properly harnessed will allow everyone to benefit from the experience." McCann faces the monumental challenge of harnessing the talents of the company's more than 1,200 employees.

Fostering the 'Contact' Economy

"I like the florist industry because I'm in the business, as I was as a social worker, of fostering contacts. We help people make contacts every day. Every person has contact points or emotional nerve endings. When one person identifies and then reaches out to make contact with another, that's the contact economy. It's a powerful force in our lives."

McCann recounts the story of a Brooklyn woman who called 1-800-FLOWERS just before Christmas and explained that she had not spoken to her sister-in-law in nearly five years, despite the fact they were next-door neighbors.

In an effort to break the silence, she ordered a floral arrangement for her sister-in-law to arrive on Dec. 23. On Christmas Eve, as the women were leaving their respective houses they bumped into each other. Hugs and apologies were exchanged and the families shared Christmas together.

Getting Involved in People's Lives

It might sound schmaltzy, but McCann says stories like that stoke his desire to be not only the world's biggest, but best, florist. "It's fun, but it's also serious business. By that I mean being a part of people's lives in a meaningful way.

"I like the challenge of getting a team of wonderful people together and charging them with goals and responsibilities. My job is to be the coach and the prodder and the instigator.

"Then at the end of the day, just when we think we're close to our goal, I raise the bar. The whole thing began with a cute idea, that is, a phone number that was the same as the company. Now, it's an internationally recognized brand name, because we were unwilling to accept the industry's status quo.

"Our goal is to make the ordinary extraordinary. Even though we are a much larger organization, I think we're actually a better organization because we have more resources on which to base our decisions. An organization can't go on forever relying on the instincts of a bootstrap entrepreneur. You can only be that lucky for so long."

VIKING OFFICE PRODUCTS

The traditional stationery store has the personal service small businesses shopping for office supplies appreciate. The warehouse-style discounters such as Office Max or Staples have the low prices.

Viking Office Products believes it has the best of both worlds, even though it chooses not to match the rock-bottom prices of the warehouses nor offer the nose-to-nose intimacy of the local office supply store.

As a direct marketer, Viking has no storefronts, no sales people. That's never stopped it, however, from providing "fanatical" customer service for businesses of up to 100 employees that are increasingly turning to the direct channel. The channel itself isn't new, it's just been reinvented by Irwin Helford, chairman, president and CEO of Los Angeles-based Viking.

The office supply superstores, which have placed the corner stationery stores on the endangered species list, are a meaningful, but manageable, source of competition for Viking.

Devastating the Stationery Stores

"The superstores have pretty well devastated the stationers and they've hurt other mail-order companies like Viking. But they haven't slowed our growth significantly. We continue to grow in the double digits," says Helford, noting that U.S. revenue growth has averaged about 17 percent over the past five years.

Even more impressive is Viking's 21 percent average return on equity in that period. Big dogs like Office Depot and Staples had average ROI's in that period of 12 percent and 9 percent, respectively.

When he took over the company in 1984, Viking's sales were stagnating at $15 million a year. Today, the global company's revenues top $800 million and analysts are predicting $1 billion in sales by the end of 1996.

What's going on at Viking?

For starters, Viking has mastered the oxymoronic task of personalizing mass marketing. Its methods include:

■ **Creating specialized catalogs to appeal to every segment in its market.** Viking produces 73 different four-color catalogs to sell more than 7,000 kinds of office supplies—everything from thumbtacks to executive credenzas. A typical buyer is a secretary, office manager or department head at a small company.

Need a new stenographer's chair? Viking has a specialty catalog for furniture. There are specialty catalogs for computer supplies, printing supplies and computer supplies.

About 75 percent of the company's sales are general office supplies, 15 percent are computer supplies and 10 percent office furniture. Viking buys its products in large volume at discounted prices directly from manufacturers.

■ **Managing a proprietary database of customers**. With virtuoso-like skill, Viking orchestrates its computerized database of 1.5 million customers by personalizing the catalogs to meet an individual's buying pattern.

As Helford explains in the company's 1994 annual report: "Our proprietary database marketing programs help us to understand and 'talk' to one customer at a time while marketing to millions."

Personalized catalogs offer "private sales" of a particular product for a specific customer, based on information Viking has dutifully squirreled away in its database since 1984, the year Helford was lured away from Reliable Corporation, a privately held, Chicago-based competitor.

"We know a lot about our customers' purchasing habits, including the recency, frequency and amount of purchases, the size of the company, their SIC (Standard Industrial Code), the number of employees, as well as other regional and demographic information that we have captured.

"We have a pretty good feel for what interests our customers. We don't want to waste their time with junk mail. We target them with offerings we know they will want," says Helford, who acknowledges that Viking pioneered the sophisticated use of database marketing in the $100 billion office products category.

"We had a head start, but certainly everyone else is catching on," says the soft-spoken Helford. From its database, Viking sent a whopping 120 million catalogs to customers and prospects in 1995. Viking's command of technology allows it to apply personal messages to most catalogs. The catalogs are all produced in-house.

Some customers receive two or three catalogs a week, according to Helford. "The object is not to bore them, so we try to make each catalog look as different as possible." In addition to its 500-page general catalog, there are 72-page specialty catalogs and 6-by-9-inch envelopes packed with 48 coupons and tabloids produced on newsprint to convey a sense of low price.

Viking obtains names of prospective customers through the rental of some 300 mailing lists that include subscribers to business publications, business seminar attendees and buyers' lists of non-competing direct mail companies.

■ **Putting a face on the catalogs.** The cover of every Viking catalog features Helford's broad smile. "People like to buy from people. Catalogs are a rather cold way to sell, but having a person identi-fied—in this case, me—helps personalize the company.

"I believe you need someone real who sticks their neck out with guarantees and promises of quality and outstanding customer ser-vice. I want them to know that I'm the person to call with a problem or a suggestion. I respond to every one of them.

"My picture helps differentiate us from the competition. If you take the good companies and their catalogs, cut off the company name and laid them side-by-side, you'd have a hard time knowing which catalog belongs to which company."

Helford's prominently displayed photo on the catalogs helps Viking build brand identity, an expensive task normally done through print and broadcast advertising. Viking doesn't spend a penny on advertising. It does its talking though its catalog and its customer service, regarded as the best in its field.

■ **Attracting customers through promotional pricing.** "Our prices are slightly higher than the superstores," says Helford. "We never intended to be and probably never will be the lowest-priced player in the field.

"We have what we call 'variable pricing,' which we developed many years ago. We will often sell the same product at different prices in different markets at the same time."

The idea is to get the prospect's or customer's attention with a price that makes favorite items attractive.

"We are the lowest priced when we choose to be. On those prod-ucts that are most important to a customer, we will be as competi-tive as anyone else. We have learned that generally people buy the first time because of price. But we're convinced that it's not price that keeps customers but service. Price is only one part of the merchandising formula."

The arrival of the office products superstore in 1986 "has created a greater awareness of price and reduced everyone's margins. It makes it tougher for everyone, but it made our business more efficient. The end-result is that the customer wins and that's the way it should be.

"Those who can better impress the customers and service them and manage their business efficiently within tighter margins will be the winners."

Viking's customer service initiatives include:

- Same day or next-day free delivery of all orders of $25 or more. In the seven U.S. cities where Viking has distribution centers, orders placed by 11 a.m. are fulfilled that afternoon. In other cities, delivery takes place by the following day.
- "If you don't like what you bought, we'll come by and pick it up for free. No questions asked," says Helford.
- 30-day trial on all products.
- A one-year guarantee, which is in addition to the manufacturer's warranty.

A Goal of Impressing Customers

"We don't think of ourselves as a commoditized business," says Helford. "The object is to impress customers so that they buy again and again."

Viking is apparently doing a good job in that regard. Its 70 percent customer retention is among the highest in the industry. Most marketers consider 50 percent a good retention rate, which means they lose as many customers as they keep.

Keeping a customer requires good listening skills. "Being a direct marketer that fields 35,000 orders a day, we're talking to customers 12 hours a day and 6 hours on Saturdays. That gives the customers convenient opportunities to tell us what we are doing wrong and how we can make it better. We have a lot of response devices: letters, postcards and callbacks."

Retention is paramount to a relationship marketer like Viking and that's why Helford is so proud of its 70 percent retention rate, a figure that is 10 percentage points higher since he joined the company. As any good marketer knows, it's four to five times less expensive to keep a customer than it is to prospect a new one.

Losing Money on New Accounts

"We analyze every piece of our business and I can tell you that we make no profit whatsoever on a new account. We actually lose money when we acquire a new account, but we weigh that against their future "lifetime value" to achieve profitability."

Retaining a customer ultimately falls in the hands of the employee and Helford says Viking is fortunate to have a work force with a compassion for the customer. "The customer can sense that, and that's what our business is all about."

As an example of customer service that goes beyond the pale, Helford cites the case of a British customer who forgot to order some labels for an important mailing. The customer was planning to travel by train from Edinburgh, Scotland, to London, where documents were to be finalized and then mailed.

Not long before boarding the train, the customer realized he didn't have the labels and in desperation called Viking's distribution center in Leicester, England. The Viking customer service representative told the customer there was no way to get the labels to Edinburgh in time.

A Race Against Time

The Viking employee, however, had a solution. As the train had to pass through Leicester on its way to London, the employee agreed to bring the labels to the station. She instructed the customer to press his Viking catalog against the window. When the train stopped, she passed the box of labels through the window. The labels were on the house, says Helford, who adds that Viking undoubtedly won a customer for life.

"We want to be judged not by what we say but by what we do. We don't make promises that we can't keep. Whatever we say in our catalog about a product or service, we'll do for the customer or we won't say it. We try very hard to care about a customer. If we have to throw out the rule book to do it then that's OK."

Growing From California Roots

Viking was founded in 1960 by Rolf Ostern as an office products supplier for California companies. The company went public in 1990. That same year, Viking established its first international beachhead in the United Kingdom. It has already become the single largest direct marketer of office products in the U.K. with sales of more than $200 million. Viking invaded France in 1992 and Australia in 1993. In 1994, Belgium, Luxembourg, the Netherlands, and Ireland were added. More countries will be added to the roster, Helford assures.

Extending the company's success into international markets was the result of "listening to the customers as we have done in the U.S. to determine the brands and the products they want and the kinds of services it would take to earn their business. We can't use a cookie-cutter approach, because each country has different tastes."

Viking has two distribution centers in the United Kingdom and one each in Australia and France. The overseas markets were attractive because the competition was less intense, although Staples had opened about a dozen stores in the United Kingdom. More U.S.-based competition may also be on the way, Helford suspects.

A Country-by-Country Strategy

Helford is confident small businesses in Europe and Australia will continue to find Viking's brand of service-intensive direct marketing appealing. Helford has certainly learned what it takes to differentiate his outfit from the superstores.

It wasn't long after assuming his post at Viking that the discount office products superstores marched onto the scene. "I admit to falling into the conventional wisdom of the time that the superstores weren't going to make it. Their financial model didn't seem do-able.

"The second round of thinking was that because they were public companies, the plan was for them to get as much as they could from the investing public and then bail out. I was wrong. In the succeeding years, everyone realized that the superstores were providing something that the customers really did want. That, after all, is what business is all about."

Realizing that the superstores were here to stay, Helford worked to reinvent the direct channel as an alternative. But he's never been fixated on what the superstores are doing.

"Our success or failure is going to be based on what we do, not what they do. If we win and grow, it's because of our accomplishments. Our future is in our hands."

NOR'WESTER BREWERY AND PUBLIC HOUSE

In the increasingly competitive field of microbrewed beer, Nor'Wester Brewery and Public House has developed a novel ingredient that's put a frothy head on sales of its Nor'Wester beer—feet on the street.

Investors in the brewery are anything but silent partners, says Jim Berneau, Nor'Wester's founder and president. "Our shareholders provide research and lead generation, help with product development and production. They serve on tasting panels and staff the facility. At the minimum, each shareholder has Nor'Wester business cards with marketing and selling messages on the back."

Nor'Wester's 8,000 business card-carrying shareholders fan out across Oregon "to present our story in the most powerful way possible," says Berneau, whose microbrewery is on the banks of the Willamette River in Portland, Oregon. "Our shareholders simply say: 'We make a great product, you might want to try it.'"

To meet the surging demand driven by their door-to-door campaign, Nor'Wester built a second brewhouse in 1995 in order to double production. In 1994, Nor'Wester's first full year of operation, it sold more than 15,000 barrels of Nor'Wester. Most microbreweries sell less than 3,000 barrels in their first year.

A Brand in Demand

"I've had restaurateurs call me and say: 'This is the sixth time I've received a business card from one of your shareholders. Maybe I better have you call on me.'"

Unlike sales reps blithely making the rounds, Nor'Wester's shareholders pitch their product to bars, restaurants and grocery stores with an almost evangelical zeal. "Our founders (shareholders) are very involved in the product from the start. They pour their creativity and enthusiasm into the company because they have a stake in the ownership," says Berneau. He doesn't need to organize sales rallies or dangle promises of all-expense paid luxury cruises to motivate his marketers. "It's a virtual volunteer army."

There are no commissions for shareholders who convince merchants to begin serving or selling Nor'Wester. There's only the satisfaction of building a brand from the grassroots, not to mention building shareholder equity. Selling microbrewed or "craft" beer is no easy task in the Great Northwest, a hotbed of microbrewed beer, where the consumer's palate is sophisticated. Good taste is a given.

That's why Berneau has sought to gain a competitive edge by reinventing the way microbrewed beer is marketed. In short, Berneau's recipe for outmarketing the competition calls on him to:

- place shareholder/owners at every point in the product distribution chain;
- ensure that the product is as fresh as can be by not filtering it in the brewing process and then move it quickly into distribution; and
- expand into other cities by building separate breweries and

inviting the public to buy shares and participate in the company's sales, marketing and product development.

Launching a Brewery

Berneau's microbrewing venture began in 1993 when he sold the public about half of the stock in Nor'Wester for $2.4 million. The share price of the initial public offering was $1.20 and shares in a secondary offering went as high as $4.20, according to Berneau. The shares don't yet pay dividends.

Nor'Wester shares aren't available on any stock exchange. Rather, they are traded among individual stockholders who use a company-provided list of potential buyers.

"For companies that choose to go this way, be warned that it is complicated. Everything has to go through the Securities and Exchange Commission," says Berneau. After his company was profiled in a national business publication, Berneau says he received phone calls from from business people in countries like Germany and Japan who wanted to learn more about his gameplan. He eagerly obliged.

Learning Lessons in College

Berneau first learned the beer business while he was the president of the student body at the University of Oregon. The student body president was ultimately responsible for the operation of a student-run cooperative store and a beer garden at the student union. "That's where I first began developing ideas for consumer-oriented programs," says Berneau. Later, he served for nine years as the director of the Oregon chapter of the National Federation of Independent Business.

Of Nor'Wester's 8,000 shareholders, about 300 are directly involved in the company's sales, marketing and product development. Those 300 are required to take a class and obtain a license from the Oregon Liquor Control Commission. The class is $30 and the license is $35, which the shareholder pays of out of his or her own pocket.

Nor'Wester does pay for the shareholder's business cards. The more than $40,000 spent on the cards is money well-spent, says Berneau, because the cards support face-to-face marketing, which packs more punch than advertising. Like most microbreweries, Nor'Wester forgoes heavy promotional spending.

Creating a Captive Audience

Nor'Wester, after all, has a captive audience of sorts because its shareholders are often the company's best customers. "You'd be amazed how much business we do selling our products to our shareholders. We have a holiday gift pack program. Shareholders buy the beer and in turn give them to their friends as presents," says Berneau.

Nor'Wester's shareholders include Anheuser-Busch, Miller and Coors distributors and their employees, figuring that, if they have a stake in Nor'Wester's success, the middlemen will help push the microbrew's sales. Berneau isn't concerned that the distributors make their money selling the major "industrial" brands like Bud or Miller, because they are not Nor'Wester's competition.

He's more concerned that "at each distribution point, we have shareholders handling the product." There's no better way to build brand loyalty.

Facing the Competitors

His competitors are local microbrews and nationally distributed craft beers such as Samuel Adams, Anchor Steam, Pete's Wicked Ale and Red Hook.

"People have a choice between us and the big craft beers. We have the distinction of being an unfiltered beer brewed down the street. In our business, the freshness of the product is critical. The closer you are to your customer, the better the opportunity the consumer has of getting a great product. You couldn't sell an unfiltered beer across the country because it would spoil."

Because Nor'Wester has only a 120-day shelf life, Nor'Wester turns to area beer distributors that in turn fulfill orders at the retail level. "Our product is very time-sensitive. It has to be cared for under perfect conditions. Beer distributors have the delivery service frequency and cold storage facilities for our product."

Brewing an Expansion Plan

Nor'Wester is sold only in the Portland area; but Berneau is broadening his distribution to such cities as Seattle, Denver and Irvine, California, where he will sell locally brewed microbeers under separate brand names. The new microbreweries will operate under the holding company Willamette Valley Inc., which is 85 percent controlled by Berneau.

Long-range, Berneau would like to brew and market beer from major cities across the U.S. "But we'll only do it from separate breweries. That's the way beer was produced many years ago."

In Seattle, where Nor'Wester began building a microbrewery in 1995, the beverage will be sold as Aviator Ale. In Irvine, the brew will be known as Bayhawk™ Ale, and in Denver, Timberline Ales.

A Recipe Unto its Own

Each brew will have its own recipe, but the business formula used in Portland will be replicated in the other cities. There are 3,500 shareholders in Seattle and about 3,000 in Denver. "The companies are separately led by their own board of directors," says Berneau. "The marketing style will differ from city to city, because of each city's unique nature."

Berneau acknowledges that some of his fellow craft brewers in the Northwest have been critical of his tactics. They've said his marketing-driven operation undermines the charm of the business.

He was even labeled "Microbrew's Bad Boy" by a Portland newspaper. Berneau finds it all laughable. "I don't think the bad boy image fits me very well," says Berneau.

Business for Everyone

"I guess we move so fast that we make our competitors a little nervous. I don't think that the art of brewing a craft beer should be reserved to just an elite few. Our concept is really like a 'people's' brewery." With America's thirst growing for craft beers, Berneau is convinced there's enough business to go around for everyone. "I don't think we need to be in each others' faces."

The "Bad Boy" image notwithstanding, Berneau is not about to begin needling his competitors. He's not above poking a little fun at his own company.

As a tongue-in-cheek gesture to the "Bad Boy" article, Berneau and some of his employees appeared at a local brewing festival in the summer of 1994 wearing black T-shirts stating "We Bad."

"We even ran the Jolly Roger up the flagpole outside our brewhouse. Maybe it's not so bad for our business because our cup has been full ever since. In the beer business, being the 'bad boy' is good business," he said with a chuckle.

Catering to the Community

Berneau is hardly a plundering pirate. "Our business is owned by the consumer and they expect their business to be a contributor to the community. We have no choice but to reflect their values." Nor'Wester, for example, donates free beer and wine to charitable organizations' fund-raising events.

Nor'Wester is affiliated with one of Oregon's largest wineries, known as Willamette Valley Vineyards Inc. Launched by Berneau in 1989, the winery underwrote a $4 million expansion several years later by selling stock from booths at area wine festivals and fairs. The winery has about 3,000 shareholders.

Berneau's public service initiatives aren't completely altruistic, because the charity events are an excellent venue to meet new customers and introduce them to beer and wine products from Nor'Wester and Willamette Valley Vineyards. He has also allowed athletic clubs, environmental clubs and other organizations to hold meetings in Nor'Wester Brewery and Public House, and Willamette Valley Vineyards facilities.

Working in the Vineyards

As with his brewery, the shareholders are invited to actively participate in the winery's operations. They pitch in by harvesting the grapes, bottling the wine and then delivering it in their own vehicles. Like the brewery, there's no compensation, no commissions, although their labors help build the equity of the company.

"We integrate out customer, to the greatest extent possible, into every phase of our business. Because consumers know how best to meet their needs, we link them directly with the operations.

"I believe that the consumer is genuinely interested in participating in a business. It's a different, but very powerful way, to market."

SECOND BAPTIST CHURCH

If pop culture and religion are competitors—and some say they are—then religion is clearly the underdog. Surveys have shown that only about 40 percent of Americans say they attend church or synagogue.

A 1995 survey by the National Council of Churches found that membership in most of the nation's 15 largest Christian churches is stagnant.

That old-time religion is a tough sell these days as most Americans have rejected religious participation. There are exceptions to the trend, of course.

Reinventing Religion

Second Baptist Church in Houston is one of the nation's growing number of so-called "megachurches" that have reinvented the way the gospel is spread. Megachurches typically have more than 2,000 members in their congregation.

Under the direction of the Rev. H. Edwin Young, Second Baptist doesn't just proselytize, it markets by using every element of the promotional mix: billboards, TV, radio, print, public relations, direct mail and special events. It publishes a 16-page, monthly magazine titled *Excitement!*

Adopting the marketing maxim that you sell the sizzle before you sell the steak, Second Baptist has attracted a huge flock of non-churchgoers with a marketing strategy as aggressive and scrappy as any corporate underdog. It calls itself "The Fellowship of Excitement."

Appealing to the TV Generation

The church's fare minimizes the dogma, old-style hymns and the kind of "sinners in the hands of an angry God" messages that turn off a free-spirited generation raised on TV, movies, concerts and sporting events.

One of the key architects of the church's success is Reverend Young, who left a larger church in Columbia, South Carolina, to accept the challenge of a stagnant church in a booming city. Lisa Milne, who is now the church's program director, and five others moved to Houston in 1978 to assist Rev. Young in his mission of rebuilding a congregation first established in 1927. Sunday attendance at the church had sunk as low as 200 by the time they hit town.

Today, the church's membership is 22,000 and still heading skyward. It has an annual budget of $16 million and a staff of 40. More than 1,200 students attend Second Baptist's kindergarten-through-12th grade school.

Sports and More

Second Baptist's 32-acre campus has athletic facilities, including three gymnasiums and several softball diamonds, where more than 300 church-sponsored teams compete in a variety of sports. There's also a library, a television studio, a bookstore and a fitness center. Its parking lots can accommodate 2,500 cars, and shuttle buses are used on Sundays to move additional worshipers to and from off-campus parking sites.

The congregation worships in a 6,200-seat octagonal-shaped "worship center" graced by one of the world's largest pipe organs that bellows through 10,473 pipes. Spanish-speaking members and guests use headsets to hear simultaneous translation of the service.

The sanctuary, nearly half the size of St. Peter's Basilica in Rome, has also served as the stage for the church's own version of Broadway-style theater and extravagant holiday pageants. For the teens and twenties set, there is a rock music service on Sunday nights.

Delivering a Meaningful Message

"Sometimes we get carried away," admits Lisa Milne. "We have to step back and look at the best way to reach the audience. We might be drawing a lot of people to our events, but if we're not reaching them in a meaningful way then we have to redefine how we'll do it next time.

"We've been criticized by traditional churches who say we're wasting our money on all those events. We listen, but we're not paralyzed by the criticism because they are not the people we are trying to reach."

Like any successful marketer, Second Baptist has a keen sense of demographics in a city with a large population of single, "unchurched" people. "Most of our new members do not come from a Baptist background. They may have a label on them—that is, they were christened as infants—but the vast majority have never been active in a church."

Overcoming Hostility

Some are not only indifferent to religion but openly hostile. "We try to understand the reasons for their hostility. Usually, there was some event in their lives that made them feel that way. Sometimes, their concept of God is someone I wouldn't want to know either."

To reach its target audience of the "unchurched," Second Baptist casts a wide media net across greater Houston, alerting people to a special event or simply inviting them to attend a Sunday service.

The church has an annual TV advertising budget of $350,000, $175,000 which is targeted for print advertising; and an additional $175,000 for special events. There are also weekly television and radio productions.

Getting their target audience's attention is a critical first step. Here are some of the key steps in Second Baptist's marketing strategy.

■ **Special events marketing.** Second Baptist calls the pageants, parades and athletic activities the "froth." "There are all of these wild activities that are designed to attract new members as well as entertain the current ones," says Milne. "If you're active in another church, this probably would not appeal to you; but, remember, our target is the person who doesn't go to church."

Prospective members certainly must have thought they were in the wrong place when a Sunday night service was enlivened by Second Baptist's own version of "Wrestlemania." Former professional wrestler Tugboat Taylor spent six weeks teaching staff members and church deacons various holds and pratfalls that were put to the test on a regulation-sized wrestling mat in the sanctuary.

No sacrilege was intended. "The idea was to give our members something that was not only fun, but an event they would feel comfortable inviting a guest to. The whole idea is to be non-intimidating."

Second Baptist also stages an annual Christmas parade around the church, featuring brilliantly-lit floats, that brings thousands to its campus each holiday season. Its musicals and holiday pageants employ casts of hundreds.

If it sounds like Second Baptist has stolen a page from Disney, they have. Rev. Young once dispatched a team of staff members to study how the master of entertainment does it. The church delegation picked up pointers from Disney on parking and trash pickup, as well. Second Baptist's staff has also studied the management practices of large corporations like Xerox.

All the froth, Milne explains, are "hooks." "The concept is that people will come for an event or two, but they're not going to keep coming if they just stay at the froth level." That leads to the next step.

■ **Relationship marketing.** Under a common scenario, a church member invites a guest to a recreation or entertainment program. All the activities end in prayer or testimony. "A message could be individually delivered," says Milne. "It's whatever seems most appropriate. We encourage people to sit down and think things through themselves.

"We concentrate on developing a personal relationship with the potential new member. We let their backgrounds and interests determine where they go in the church." Second Baptist prefers the soft sell as many of the potential members have a natural wariness of things religious.

"There are some who may think we're going to shut the doors behind them and take all their money," said Milne, who noted that some prospective members seek reassurance that the church has nothing to do with some of the loose-cannon televangelists who created scandal in the 1980's.

Second Baptist's 18-member lay finance committee, which is headed by an oil company executive, sees to it that every dollar finds its proper place.

As new members become more involved in the church's core mission of understanding God and the Bible, "we encourage them to move back up into the froth and meet the next generation of new members."

■ **Segmenting the audience.** Second Baptist doesn't believe religion should be one-size-fits-all. "We look at all the niche markets in our society. We realize that the traditional definition of the family may not apply to the majority of people," says Milne.

"We look at where there is a need in society and create a program to meet that audience's need. We have identified hundreds of niches. For example, we have nearly 40 support groups for such things as drug or alcohol dependence, overeating, divorce, or death of a spouse." All of the programs are biblically-centered.

Second Baptist has programs for teens, Generation X-ers and senior citizens. The church has a vast array of community outreach programs that members are encouraged to participate in, including those which feed the hungry, shelter the homeless, work with disadvantaged children, and visit the sick and elderly in nursing homes. "We are involved in almost every charitable activity in Houston," says Milne.

The church attempts to match a volunteer's skills with the right community activity. "We try to direct people to where their gifts lie and what their hearts desire. For example, a person who went through a divorce may have a real heart for a child whose parents are going through a divorce. That person would be an effective counselor."

A Moving Service

As Rev. Young explained to the *New York Times*: "Church ought to be fun. Most churches you go to are boring. It's like you're captured behind the stained glass. Our service moves. There's no dead time. We're not out to teach somebody some medieval anthem."

Members of the Second Baptist Church don't join for the flash alone. Average weekly worship attendance is nearly 12,000 and more than 6,000 members attend Bible study classes held during three separate sessions on Sunday.

Second Baptist is unlike a traditional, conservative Protestant church, explains Rev. Young, "because to get to Christ you have to tunnel your way through all the religious doctrine. There's a hard, outer surface. If you're outside looking in, it's very intimidating. You have to understand the right words and phrases to get to the center of it."

'Hatching, Matching & Dispatching'

Nor is Second Baptist like a second popular style of church that Rev. Young has described as the "hatching, matching, dispatching kind of church." In that kind of church, members are focused on events such as birth, christening, marriage and burial. "It's not tightly organized on what you have to believe. Doing good deeds and loving one another is important, and Christ is talked about but is not the central focus. That type of church is more centered on society," says Young.

Second Baptist has created a third model. "Think of it as a circle drawn around a big cross," says Milne. "Around the circle is the froth and within the froth are hooks to bring people from outside into the center.

"If we look like a stained-glass fortress, there would less opportunity to involve people. We want them to recognize there is a big door in," says Young. The size of the congregation only rarely has been a turnoff for new members because they were never accustomed to the intimacy of a 300-seat church in the first place.

In a sense, there are hundreds of smaller congregations within the church in the form of softball or basketball teams, support groups, choirs and bible study groups.

Listening to the Clientele

Creating the right mix of programs for the members is not easy for a congregation as large as Second Baptist's. Despite the church's rapid growth, Rev. Young has opted to keep a lid on expenses by not expanding the staff.

"Almost every staff member teaches a bible class which allows us to get first-hand feedback from the members. We don't just wander the halls or sit in our offices. We get involved in our members' lives, which are extremely busy.

"It's the 'busy-ness' of their lives that is the real enemy to this church or any church. There are too many distractions and that's what we must compete against. But if we can provide them fun, relevant programs and get members to contemplate some of the larger issues in life like: 'Why am I here?' or 'Is there a God and how can I get to know him?' then we're accomplishing our mission."

Sometimes all it takes to get them is a little bit of underdog marketing to get the ball rolling.

CHRISTIAN SUPPLY CENTERS

If religious bookstores sound like musty, solemn places, consider what Christian Supply Centers is doing to make it the largest chain of Christian bookstores on the West Coast.

"I think we have a Disneyland gene somewhere," Gary Randall says with a laugh. The president of the Portland, Oregon-based chain of 13 stores, Randall describes the atmosphere in his stores as a "cross between Barnes and Noble and the state fair. It's not like a library at all. People are in here meeting other people. There are a lot of conversations. It's a fun place."

On any given day, visitors to the stores can find an author signing his or her latest book. Some book signings have attracted as many as 1,500 people. Performers such as musicians or dancers entertain the customers who can compete in contests for prizes. On Saturdays, there's a children's hour and various reading groups meet throughout the week. It's hardly business as usual at Christian Supply Centers.

Adding Coffee to the Mix

Wingbacked chairs invite book lovers to sink in and page through their favorite novel. Coffee may soon be added to the mix, as Randall is talking to Starbucks about opening counters in the stores.

An ordained minister and former host of a long-running Christian-oriented television show on the CBS affiliate in Portland, Randall knows that the medium is a big part of the message. "It's important how we present ourselves. That's why we have remodeled all our stores to give them airy looks. There's lots of glass. It's very open and inviting."

Christian Supply has reinvented the way a religious bookstores operates and markets itself. The company's innovative promotions and merchandising efforts have increased sales as much as 100 percent in a year in some stores.

Turning Over a New Leaf

The story at Christian Supply Centers wasn't always so upbeat. The chain of six stores operated by Portland's Multnomah Bible College had grown tired. Sales were in a slump. The stores themselves had grown shop-worn.

Randall, who had resigned his pastorship, was looking for new opportunities and believed he could breathe new life into the chain and then expand it into other West Coast cities. He approached his friend Robert B. Pamplin Jr., an ordained minister and president of R.B. Pamplin Corporation, a textile and sand and gravel mining concern that is Oregon's largest private company, with a proposal to buy Christian Supply.

"I told him we could bring a higher level of energy and marketing ability to the organization," says Randall.

"Bob said he thought the idea sounded great but he didn't think the chain was for sale. It wasn't; but I told him I might be able to talk the college into selling because I knew they had been having some financial problems with the stores." After talking to several of the college's trustees, Randall learned that they would entertain an offer for the stores.

The Birth of a Publishing Venture

The idea was born and the deal went through in December, 1993. In 1994, Christian Supply Centers, Inc., started Pamplin Entertainment in the Christian market, a company which will soon also be headed by Randall. The company is developing a video series for children for distribution.

For Pamplin's bookstore investment to pay off, Christian Supply would have to begin doing business with much more flair to stand out in Portland, home to 48 other Christian bookstores.

Under Randall's direction, Christian Supply took several key steps to outmarket the competition, including:

■ **Presenting a new and broader line of merchandise.** Under the previous ownership, nearly everything sold at Christian Supply was religious books and bibles. Today, only about 40 percent of its sales comes from books and bibles.

"We began carrying the top line of gifts from the major gift marts in places like Seattle and Atlanta," says Randall. Christian Supply added such products as the Precious Moments porcelain fig-urines of cherub-faced children to the dramatic landscape paintings of Thomas Kinkade, whose works command retail prices as high as $6,000.

"You can now find anything you would expect to see in a nice boutique at a resort," says Randall. "We took a big step up in Chris-tian retailing." The line of giftware also features many lower-priced items. Much of the merchandise is not specifically Christian in nature, he notes. For example, the stores sell wooden carvings of rainbow and brook trouts.

Gifts constitute about 22 percent of the chain's sales. An even larger component of Christian Supply's receipts, about 27 percent, comes from the sale of religious music in the form of compact disks, tapes or sheet music. A small but growing percentage of sales is gen-erated through the sale of Christian-oriented videotapes.

The merchandise is intended to appeal to both Christian and general audiences, says Randall. Christian Supply has 35 divisions of books, including Christian fiction, marriage and the family, to Biblical prophecy and a section devoted to Messianic Jewish literature.

■ **Launching an advertising campaign on radio.** "Even though I come from a television background, we do no television advertising, although we may consider it in 1996," says Randall. About 90 per-cent of its advertising budget goes to buy spots on not only the local Christian radio station, but on stations with talk, news, and country and western formats.

Because his recognition level is high from his 12 years on local television, Randall is the company's radio spokesman. For the first eight to ten months after Pamplin Publishing bought Christian Supply, the radio spots were aired only on Christian stations.

"After that market became saturated, our spots were heard on every major radio station in town. People were astounded that a Christian operation was advertising so heavily in the general marketplace, but we have a line of merchandise that appeals to everyone," says Randall. One way to expose a broad audience to Christian literature, he adds, is to get the general public to come in and browse or attend a special event.

About 10 percent of Christian Supply's advertising budget is spent on ads in local newspapers.

■ **Enhance the company's image through a major remodeling of the stores.** By giving its stores a cleaner, more modern look, Randall says Christian Supply sends a strong signal to the marketplace that things have changed.

"Marketing and image will lead the way," says Randall. "People will follow if they sense a new spirit and look, but they will soon fall away if you don't have the product and the value."

To ensure that it had a broad line of merchandise, Christian Supply increased the size of its flagship store by about 50 percent. "I don't think any one element will make or break a sales organization. Everything makes a contribution such as our remodeled stores, better merchandising and our advertising messages."

No Longer an Underdog

Once an underdog, Christian Supply has captured about 50 percent of the Christian books and merchandise market in Portland. Christian Supply's competitors, mostly small independent stores, have not reacted with alarm or attempted to retaliate.

The higher visibility for Christian books and merchandise generated by Christian Supply's marketing campaign has lifted the sales of nearly every store in the area. "I'm not sure what they're saying about us in their prayers, but the competitors have said they've benefited from our broad-based advertising. One owner, however, told me that we are hurting him. That's not a joyful thing for me. I'm sorry about that."

Although he doesn't enjoy the cutthroat element of marketing competition, Randall enjoys the thrill of creating and expanding a new business. "We're now getting calls from people all over the country who have heard about the success of the chain and want to come to work for us." Christian Supply's in-store sales people are not highly paid, but they are highly motivated through a series of bonuses, says Randall.

An Award-Winning Store

The Christian Booksellers Association, in the spring of 1995, designated Christian Supply's flagship store as the "store of the year" for the Northwest Region and one of the top 10 stores in the country. The award is based on several criteria, including sales growth, merchandising, marketing, accounting practices, employee training, customer service and store appearance.

The Christian retailing business in general has been on the rise in recent years. "People are swinging from a materialistic to a more spiritual and personal growth mentality," says Randall. "They are looking to Christianity as well as other religions for certain needs in their lives."

Wall Street, a place not known for its spirituality, has taken note of the growth in Christian retailing, says Randall. "The investment community recognizes that companies like ourselves are poised to do big business in the years ahead."

Tackling New Markets

Christian Supply opened two new stores beyond the six original stores it inherited from the previous ownership. The chain then targeted the Seattle market where it has already opened five stores. The company is trending toward opening larger stores than the average Christian bookstore.

As it was before its re-launch in Portland, Christian Supply is an underdog in Seattle. It has only a tiny share of the Christian retail market. Family Bookstores, a 200-store Christian book chain, is the leading Christian bookseller in that market with about 10 stores.

"We don't have a dominant position up there, but we're confident customers will find our new style and approach to Christian retailing appealing," says Randall. The same customer-driven formula that's worked so well in Portland will play equally as well in the larger metropolitan area of Seattle.

"Marketing is everything as far as I'm concerned."

5 The Perfecters

One way for an underdog to outmarket the competition is to take an element in its marketing mix and perfect it to the point where it can't be matched. That could be the company's product development strategy, its distribution, its customer service strategies or its inventory management.

Computer City has done a lot of things right in its rapid rise to become the nation's No. 2 computer retailer behind CompUSA. Thanks to an investment in and a commitment to a sophisticated inventory management system, Computer City can meticulously manage every item in its store.

Upstart Computer City was able to seriously challenge CompUSA, the reigning computer retailing king, which, in 1993, got tripped by a lack of cost and inventory control in its nationwide chain of stores. CompUSA has righted its ship and has redoubled its efforts to fend off aggressive competitors like Computer City. Alan Bush, president of Computer City, says his store's underdog success owes little to luck, but a great deal to "very good execution of the basic rules."

While Dell Computer ventured into the retail channel, Gateway 2000 stayed home to cultivate and perfect its selling techniques in the direct channel. Gateway's stick-to-the-knitting distribution strategy helped it overtake Dell as the nation's largest direct seller of personal computers. Dell later abandoned the retail channel.

Pennsylvania's Meridian Bancorp has perfected the use of computer technology to gain an edge in its highly competitive marketplace where four larger banks compete. Computerization not only allows to Meridian to replicate the brand of personal service it provided in the 1950's when it was a small bank, but also helps it to better identify and meet the needs of its best retail and commercial customers.

Allen-Edmonds' shoes grace the feet of leading men from Hollywood to the White House. Why such a loyal following among America's Who's Who? A perfectly produced pair of shoes is a good place to start. The company's craftsmen painstakingly march the shoes through a 212-step manufacturing process. A high-quality product has become Allen-Edmonds' stock in trade.

Now, meet the Perfecters.

COMPUTER CITY

Midway through a telephone interview, Alan Bush, president of Computer City, apologized for having to take an urgent call. Returning a couple of minutes later, Bush explained he was talking to one of his store managers in Florida.

Bush had queried the manager after being called by a customer who wasn't completely satisfied with her shopping experience at the Computer City store. "The interesting thing is that the customer was my sister," says Bush, who shared that fact with his manager.

"I told him: 'Now that I have told you what I have heard, I assume you're not going to tell me that the customer is a liar,'" says Bush. "Actually things are in very good shape at that store and my sister left with a very nice computer system. I told the manager we could do just a little better."

Opening 100 Stores

Doing things a little better has helped Computer City become the nation's No. 2 computer retailer, with more than $2 billion in sales. Market leader CompUSA has about 85 stores and more than $2.8 billion in fiscal 1995 sales.

By the end of 1995, Fort Worth, Texas-based Computer City said it hopes to surpass its larger archrival in terms of outlets by opening its 100th store. It began the year with 70.

Van Baker, an analyst for the market research firm, Dataquest, told *Business Week,* "It wouldn't surprise me if CompUSA is the No. 2 computer superstore two years from now."

Becoming the No. 1 computer retailer would be quite a feat for Computer City, which didn't even open its first store until the Christmas season of 1991. Computer City, a division of retail powerhouse Tandy Corporation, is said to be the second company to reach $1 billion in sales in three years or less. The only company to reach that plateau quicker was Sam's Club, a unit of Wal-Mart.

Growing fast and getting it right seem almost contradictory, but Computer City has pulled it off by perfecting several critical marketing elements that have tripped up competitors.

Red Tide Rising

Computer superstore pioneer CompUSA saw its once-robust growth stall in 1993 when its inventory management problems began to mount. The 80-store, Dallas-based chain, slipped into the red before returning to profitability in late 1994. The price of its stock was again soaring in 1995. But, while this cross-town competitor was wrestling with its inventory management nightmare in 1993, Computer City was perfecting its inventory control system.

Computer City's inventory control is now so good that it doesn't even need a warehouse. All merchandise is shipped on a just-in-time basis to its stores in the U.S., Canada and Europe.

"Most of the gains that can be made on gross margins on products are the result of how well you manage your inventory once it's inside your building," says Bush. "We spend a tremendous amount of time trying to make certain that we have a very low cost of operation.

"We have tight inventory controls. It's one of the fundamentals of this business. It's pretty obvious that others in this exciting segment are learning the importance of inventory management. Tandy's Chairman and CEO John V. Roach says that Computer City may sell a lot of glamorous products, but it's really not a very glamorous business. It's retail execution at its finest and that's what a lot of this business is—very good execution of the basic rules."

Keeping a Lid on Costs

One of the key steps that Computer City took to keep its distribution costs low was to initiate a bar-coding program that allows the stores to track every unit from the factory to the day it is sold. "It also allows us to keep the latest version of a product on our shelves. If a software vendor says they're coming out with version 4.0 and they want to take back version 3.0, we know exactly how many versions of each we have in every store."

Perfecting inventory management wasn't as easy at it sounds. "Although we're in a very high-tech industry, we found there were a lot of low-tech suppliers. Very few of the manufacturers actually shipped us bar-coded products."

That was until Bush, who admits he can be "a little aggressive when necessary," got serious. The suppliers began to change their ways. A hands-on administrator, Bush often works directly with suppliers. He once told IBM that they needed to change the look of the packaging for a personal computer product, because he thought it hurt the product's salability. IBM adopted his suggestion.

Trotting the Globe

On the day of this interview, the fast-moving Bush was preparing to fly to Salt Lake City where he, along with John Roach and San Francisco 49ers quarterback Steve Young, a hometown hero from his days at Brigham Young University, were going to cut the ribbon on Computer City's newest store. From there, he was going to drop in on a competitor, The Wireless Store, and end the day by having dinner with a vendor. The following day, he was going to make a speech in New York.

People and vendors listen carefully to what Bush has to say, now that Computer City has become such a force in the computer retail channel, where four-fifths of all computers are sold. Other ingredients to Computer City's success include:

■ **Creating a pleasant customer experience.** "We've got a good understanding of the customer," says Bush. "We talk to the customer leaving our competitors' stores and we talk to customers in our stores or other Tandy stores like Incredible Universe and Radio Shack.

"What we've learned is that the customer didn't mind spending money. What the customer really hated was the shopping experience. The customer didn't like working with commissioned sales people, so we went with non-commissioned sales people. The customers also said they didn't like getting to the checkout counter where they were attacked by the '800-pound gorilla' standing there trying to sell them an extended service plan.

"All of those things combined to make the customer's experience very difficult in our competitors' stores. That's why we changed it."

To ensure that customers get a fair shake in the store, Computer City uses a mystery shopping service, which sends a representative to all of its stores about twice per quarter.

"They ask our associates questions, buy products and in some cases return them to see how well they are treated," says Bush.

Sales people can qualify for company incentive programs based on how well they are scored by a mystery shopper. Managers' bonuses and qualification for incentives, such as cruises and trips to leisure destinations, are based on the level of customer service rendered by them and their employees.

Because Computer City recognizes customer service as critical to its success, Bush installed the company's customer service coordinator in the office next to his. "She keeps me informed as to where we are not exceeding our customer's expectations. Customer satisfaction is measured not by how we think the customer was treated; it's how the customers think they were treated that really matters.

"The term 'world-class customer service' is a registered trademark of Computer City and we're going to live up to that by getting a constant stream of customer feedback. We have comment cards that provide for direct feedback from the customers. My name is posted on the card. It reminds our sales associates that our customers always have an additional course of action."

■ **Competitive pricing.** Each Computer City store sends a team around each week to compare prices at competitors' stores. If pricing discrepancies are found, says Bush, the buying group is notified and prices are adjusted. The company has a policy of matching a competitor's low price.

■ **Brand names strategy.** "We are first and foremost a brand name house," says Bush, who notes that Computer City carries more than a dozen leading brands of computers.

"You can go to a lot of our competitors that advertise a lot of brand names, but the sales associates are incented to sell a house-brand computer that has a higher profit margin for the store," he says. "That's not fair to the customers nor to our vendors."

Computer City has a house-brand computer called U.S. Logic (Canadian Logic for stores north of the border). Sales associates are not given incentives to push the brand, which constitutes only about 5 percent of the chain's sales.

"We don't really want to be in the in-house brand business. But one of the things we have learned over the years is that our vendors don't always have supplies on a timely basis or in the configurations our customers want. The U.S. Logic brand gives us that flexibility."

Brand names are what drive Computer City. "We thought it was critical that the customer had a place to go where they could see, hear and feel all the leading brands of computers under one roof." Computer City has more than 5,000 items in stock, which, besides computers, include software, printers and office furniture.

■ **Comparative advertising.** Occasionally, Computer City runs a series of print ads in newspapers comparing its prices with CompUSA's as well as with other competitors such as Microcenter, Fry's and Best Buy.

■ **Managers with major retailer experience.** Computer City recruits many of its managers from leading retailers such as Wal-Mart, K-mart, Toys R Us and Best Buy. "We go after the best, most experienced talent available. You have to have good people working with you or the plan will never work."

Managers had better stay on their toes. Bush, as well as most of the headquarters group, has a habit of turning up at Computer City stores all over the world on short notice.

■ **Long-range planning.** "We think a lot of mistakes our competitors have made are the result of knee-jerk reactions. We're really not interested in knee-jerk reactions. The Tandy Corporation Board of Directors has approved our five-year plan. We have a good plan and we stick with it," says Bush.

The company's marketing strategies and expansion plans are mapped out in these five-year plans that are updated once a year. "In the summer of 1995, for example, we updated it through the year 2000. We don't deviate from the plan." By the year 2000, the company projects it will be operating more than 200 stores in the U.S. and abroad.

The company plans to continue to expand into English-speaking countries and into major cities within North America.

Summoned From Down Under

Bush says he had no idea he would ever be the president of a $2 billion company—at least not until 1991. While in Australia that year hosting a Radio Shack sales incentive trip, he received a call from his daughter who instructed him to call John Roach.

"When I reached him, he told me I needed to meet him at Dallas-Forth Worth International Airport on Monday. He wouldn't give me any details. I said I'd like to meet him there, but it was Sunday in Australia. He said that was not a problem because it was only Saturday in Dallas."

Bush grabbed the first available flight to Los Angeles with a connection to DFW. "I got there by Monday, but John was not there. He had to go somewhere else. But he left me some documents with the code name: Project Antelope."

Tapped for the Job

Bush spent the rest of the week studying the plans that helped lay the groundwork for what would become Computer City. The following Saturday, Roach visited Bush at his office and asked him if he wanted to be involved in the project. "I asked him how soon he needed an answer. He said: 'I don't. You started last Saturday.' "

It was a great leap forward for Bush, who signed on with Tandy in 1976 when he became a manager/trainer in Nashua, New Hampshire, after he graduated from college. He rose to the position of divisional vice president of Radio Shack, a post he held for only eight months before being tapped for the presidency of Computer City.

A Curiosity on Wall Street

Although Computer City doesn't have to go hat in hand to Wall Street, analysts on the Street are extremely interested in what Computer City has to say. "Analysts want to learn more about us because Computer City provides a unique window into the performance of many high-tech vendors like Apple Computer, IBM and Compaq. Securities analysts welcome the opportunity to talk to a retailer handling their products."

In case the analysts were wondering, Bush says Computer City aims for a 3 percent pre-tax profit. "If we can't generate a return to Tandy's investors then we don't deserve to be in business. We're happy to be profitable in a business where so many others are struggling for profitability. And, while profitability is essential to any business, sustained profitability and revenue growth have been the hallmark of Tandy Corporation for quite some time."

One of the real strengths of Computer City, he says, is that the management team is focused on running the business. "Our management team doesn't have to worry about much of the corporate responsibilities. Tandy Corporation does that on behalf of all its divisions."

Close Bonds With the Parent

His relationship with Roach and Tandy's senior management is strong, says Bush. "I can go in there with any problem or brainstorm for any kind of solution with them. Computer City would not be where it is today without that kind of leadership from the chairman."

Reflecting on the inroads his compay has made against CompUSA, its larger, more-established competitor, Bush reiterates that the secret to outmarketing them was sticking to its long-range plan.

"The race is not to see who has the biggest company or who gets the golden ring first. The real measure of success is who's still in the race many miles down the road. I have a high degree of confidence that we'll be there. We just have to stick with our plan and always improve on it."

GATEWAY 2000

One way to get good at something is to stick with it. Ask Gateway 2000, the largest direct seller of personal computers in America. Marketing director Al Giazzon explains that Gateway has never strayed from the direct into the retail channel. Why let the middleman take anywhere from a 4 percent to a 10 percent cut of the profit?

Gateway's direct-selling arch rival, Dell Computer, found out the hard way that it's tough to be a successful PC marketer in both the retail and direct channels. In 1990, Dell began an ill-fated plunge into the retail channel by selling through such stores as Sam's Club and CompUSA.

By the time Dell had pulled up stakes in the retail channel in 1994, underdog Gateway, a company founded in a South Dakota farmhouse in 1985 by the then 22-year-old Ted Waitt, had raced past Dell to become the top dog in PC direct selling. Practice makes perfect.

Launching an International Front

Though Dell has a big lead over Gateway in international sales, Giazzon notes that Gateway intends to surpass Dell there, too. Gateway launched its overseas offensive with showrooms in Paris and Frankfort in 1994. That same year, Gateway began enlisting distributors in Latin America and the Far East. International revenues in 1994 were $190 million, a figure Giazzon predicts will grow substantially in the next several years.

Regardless of what country Gateway peddles its PC's in, it will only be done through phone selling, Giazzon assures. "Our secret is focus. When Dell and other PC direct marketers decided to dabble in the retail channel, Gateway stayed true. It hurt Dell, because they had absorb all the costs of doing business at retail."

Perfecting Direct Selling

In 1990, Dell held a slight edge in sales over Gateway. By concentrating on and perfecting its direct selling techniques, Gateway had captured about 27 percent of the direct PC market by the end of 1994, versus Dell's 20 percent.

Based in the decidedly un-Silicon Valley-like town of North Sioux City, South Dakota, Gateway has never been tempted by the retail channel where four out of five PC's are sold. "We've studied it. We've talked to all the retail players and we've done the math. It just doesn't work because of their take."

Cracking the Million Mark

Gateway seems to be doing fine without retail partners. In 1994, the company shipped more than 1 million computers, ranking it fifth in the U.S. in PC sales. The company, which now has more than 5,000 employees, has a streak of eight straight years of revenue growth of more than 50%.

Gateway has used several strategies to outmarket Dell and the fast-fading smaller direct-selling PC wannabes.

■ **Pricing.** Because it doesn't have to pay the retailer's markup, Gateway can sell its PC's and systems for less than leading retail-oriented PC marketers like Apple, Compaq and IBM.

In 1995, a Gateway customer spent an average of $2,600 for a fully-loaded system which includes monitor, keyboard, bundled software and a CD-ROM drive. Dell customers pay an average of $2,700 per system and prices for comparable systems sold by competitors through retail typically begin at around $3,000. Liking what it saw in the direct channel, IBM launched its own mail-order outfit called Ambra, but scrapped it in 1994.

"They couldn't keep up with Gateway," says Giazzon, who explains that IBM's direct-selling campaign was doomed by infighting between Ambra, IBM Direct and IBM. "There was too much channel conflict. The IBM sales rep didn't like it that some of their sales were being taken away by this direct unit.

"We liked it when IBM moved in on us, because it gave us another reference point. When they were in our channel, we told people to compare the value and we won on that comparison." After IBM's experience, Giazzon doesn't expect the other large PC makers to enter the channel. Compaq, Digital Equipment Corporation and Apple all have small presences in direct.

"There's been some hard lessons learned. The only new entrant might be a company from the Far East."

Gateway doesn't have a channel conflict problem, because it has no field sales representatives. Sales, driven by direct response advertising, are handled over the phone.

Gateway's pricing pattern is relatively flat across its product line, which includes desktop and laptop computers, as well as a full range of peripherals. "Some PC companies make higher margins on some products and keep the prices high for a month or two before dropping the price. Our business model says we'll maintain our margin, but as soon as we get a cost savings we lower the price."

That means when a customer is looking at the price of a system in a print ad, the stated price is higher than the actual price. "Customers like that. It helps close the sale."

■ **Educated buyers.** Gateway buyers have the confidence to buy a PC or system over the phone. They don't need to "kick the tires" at retail.

Independent and in-house research indicates that the average household income of a Gateway customer is $70,000. "Our customers have the highest household income of all PC buyers and are second only to Apple in terms of educational levels."

About 70 percent of Gateway's $2.7 billion in 1994 sales went to individuals, 30 percent to corporate buyers. Corporate decision-makers who have a Gateway at home are increasingly ordering them for the office. Often, the orders are high-volume.

"We call it the 'cul-de-sac' effect," says Giazzon. "An individual buyer becomes a reference point for us in the corporate environment." Gateway, which only began exhibiting at trade shows in 1994, wants to boost its presence in the corporate market.

It will encounter Dell at every turn in that market, which generates about half of Dell's sales. Gateway is hardly turning its back on the home market, which now generates more sales than the business market.

■ **Incorporating customer feedback.** Gateway has an in-house survey organization that is continuously taking the pulse of its customers and the PC marketplace. One of the advantages of being a direct marketer, Giazzon points out, is that Gateway deals directly with its customers. This 'bread crumb' trail to the customer doesn't grow cold as it does by going through the retail channel.

"We do customer surveys every quarter to determine what they do and do not like," says Giazzon, who notes that Gateway is extremely attentive to its installed base of customers. "We want our customers to keep coming back to us, and they do. Ninety-four percent of the people who buy a Gateway will buy again from us."

Because it talks to its customers every hour of every day, Gateway can quickly accommodate their product specifications. Components can be instantly plugged in and systems are custom-configured as the order comes in over the phone. There are no large inventories to dredge through as with the retail-oriented PC makers.

■ **Direct response advertising.** With no storefronts or sales reps in the field, Gateway relies on direct response ads in the leading PC magazines like *PC Magazine, InfoWorld* and *Computer Shopper*, a magazine so hefty that it weighs more than Gateway's four-pound Liberty laptop computer. Gateway spends about $30 million on print advertising.

Gateway's media buys were strictly print until 1994 when it began experimenting in several East Coast markets with 60-second direct response television spots created by Minneapolis ad agency Carmichael Lynch. Consumers, with their credit cards at the ready, were invited to call Gateway's toll-free number and order a PC. It arrived on the doorstep a day or two later.

Initial TV results were encouraging. "Less than 10 percent of the people who responded had called Gateway before, yet 45 percent already owned a computer" says Giazzon, who was delighted to find a new, largely untapped market.

Gateway does not try to lure Dell or the other PC makers into advertising dogfights. "We have a strong position in the desktop market. We would rather not give the competition any additional ink," says Giazzon.

The laptop market is another matter. "We do target companies like Toshiba, Dell and Compaq who have some marketshare with laptops. We compare ourselves directly with them and make the case that we're better." Gateway's new Liberty DX4-100 laptop was already back-ordered shortly after introduction, according to Giazzon.

Gateway has been aggressive about using technology to sell technology. In 1995, Gateway launched a home page on the World Wide Web, the multimedia portion of the Internet. The company also has sites on the major commercial on-line services like Prodigy and America Online.

Gateway's Web site has sections on customer service, product and price information, news releases, technical support and the top 50 questions most commonly asked by Gateway customers. The site is also an excellent feedback gathering and entertainment vehicle, says Giazzon. Gateway's presence in cyberspace is designed specifically to generate revenues.

"We don't take orders on-line, because it's still too early in terms of security," says Giazzon, noting that hackers have violated the security of other company's computers. "It's more customer-service driven at this point, because our customers like to use technology."

One unique way Gateway delivers a marketing message is through the CD-ROM drives that have become standard with every Gateway system shipped. "We have a system CD-ROM drive that has some little advertising messages on it. We also plan to begin advertising on the CD's that computer magazines are bringing out.

Unlike print advertising, we display our multimedia capabilities on those CD's."

To reinforce the loyalty of its customer base, Gateway launched its own magazine in the spring of 1995. The title "GW2k" is Gateway's sign on the Internet. The 40-page quarterly magazine carries ads from other high-tech companies like Microsoft and Intel which provide Gateway's operating system software and microchips, respectively. Don't look for any ads from Dell or Compaq, however.

The magazine or "magalog" has a small catalog of office furniture from the Turnstone Division of Steelcase Inc. and there is a section for Gateway branded apparel. One way to build a brand is to emblazon a corporate logo on baseball caps, sweatshirts and coffee cups.

The magazine's circulation is more than 1 million. "We're larger than *PC Magazine*," Giazzon says with pride. Ted Waitt gets a page in the magazine to explain where the company is headed.

"Improving tech support is our No. 1 goal. We want to have the best tech support in the industry and we will. The addition of our Kansas City facility (great city, great BBQ, great views, cool people) will enable us to do this.

"We had to face the fact—there just aren't enough people in Sioux City to properly support our growth. And, for some reason, not everyone wants to live here (OK by me, I like it small). So we've built a great team in KC (soon 1,000 strong) and you'll be the beneficiary."

"The magazine is one more way to build a bond with our customer." To further cement that bond, customers are invited to join Club Gateway. The admission price is the purchase of a Gateway system. Membership privileges include discounts on peripherals, upgrades and software packages.

■ **Creating a personality.** Proud of its Midwestern roots, Gateway's corporate logo is a cow spot. "We have a certain charm, an image that an agency can't create for you. It has something to do with the fact we're in South Dakota.

"We have a simple, recognizable personality and that's a powerful position to have in the market. I believe it's harder for people to come up with a quick sentence about Dell than it is about Gateway.

"Who comes to mind when you think of Dell? ... Michael Dell (the company's founder and chairman). We don't even try to attach Ted to the company, because we're more focused on the spirit and the personality of the company. We want to convey our Midwestern values. Value is the mainstay of our product definition.

"Although it's a subtle distinction, our brand allows us a stronger core customer group that is less likely to abandon us. They are more inclined to buy from us again," says Giazzon.

"When the press talks about what we are doing right, they say we're doing a good job of building an image and a corporate culture and communicating that through our advertising." The press also has written about how well Gateway has mastered the direct channel.

Analysts predict that by 1998, Gateway could control more than 40 percent of the direct PC market. "We'll continue to grow, because the more people become educated about computers, the more likely they are to buy direct," says Giazzon. "Comfort is the big hurdle in buying direct. Once customers have tried it, they will keep coming back. We just have to continue working at making them comfortable."

MERIDIAN BANCORP

When you run a bank with $15 billion in assets and over 300 branches spread throughout three states, it's hard to know your customers.

But thanks to advances in database technology and portable computing, relationship banking has become more than an empty promise. Technology is allowing Meridian Bancorp, one of the nation's 50 largest banking companies, to provide mass customization of its product and service offerings, which in turn leads to a virtual one-on-one relationship with its customers.

"We know more about customers than ever before," explains Samuel A. McCullough, chairman, president and CEO of Meridian Bancorp. "We are using different types of information to predict what you may or may not do." With that kind of insight into a customer's current and future needs, McCullough says Meridian can better differentiate its service in the intensely competitive Pennsylvania banking environment and prepare itself for the nationwide banking environment to come.

An Underdog on its Home Turf

Although Reading, Pennsylvania-based Meridian is one of the nation's biggest banks, it's clearly an underdog on its home turf, where four larger super-regional and regional banking companies scrap for share. The big dogs are PNC Bank Corporation with $62 billion in assets, Mellon Bank Corporation with $42 billion, First Union with $36 billion and CoreStates Financial with $30 billion.

And then there's Meridian, which McCullough says will out-market the big dogs on the strength of its personal relationships that technology will help deliver.

Through the use of technology, Meridian is perfecting the use of internal customer information combined with external data to help it identify and profile its best customers. That allows Meridian to better segment its service and create relationships in a business better known for impersonal, banker-like ways.

Re-engineering the Culture

Sue Perrotty, group executive vice president and head of retail banking and strategic market distribution, says that in 1992, Meridian "began to dramatically re-create our culture and change our information infrastructure so we could build a core competency on customer information." The program has been dubbed the "Strategic Customer Information Platform."

"We always knew how many checks a customer wrote. We were always very transactionally efficient, but we couldn't anticipate what a customer's needs would be or how to counsel them," says Perrotty. "Banks do business with everyone who walks through the door, but we had to get focused on who was the most important and make sure that we served them. We never thought that way before."

Creating New Selling Opportunities

With a better handle on a customer's checking and savings accounts, loans, asset management plans and investments, Meridian can do a better job of marketing and cross-selling its products and services. For example, when a customer presents himself or herself at a teller window, the teller can immediately call up on the screen the customer's banking history and perhaps alert the customer to a certificate of deposit that will be maturing shortly.

It allows the bank a selling opportunity and gives the customer the sense that the bank genuinely cares about the customer's investment strategies.

"We have spent a lot of money in the last two or three years to get us to the point of just knowing who the customers are and how much they produce for us in terms of profit. We now know what each product produces in profit by customer as well as what every relationship manager produces in return to the company," says McCullough.

By "data warehousing" information from various application systems in a central database, employees and customers have better access to the bank's offerings. The information is now readily available in every branch and on the laptop computers of the bank's commercial loans officers, who spend more time in the field at customer's offices than they do in their offices.

"We have a small headquarters building with not many people here," says McCullough, "If we're right about which direction both commercial and retail banking are going in the 1990's then we probably won't be building any new non-branch offices. We want our employees out in the customers' offices with their laptops."

Unleashing the Reps

A project called "Focus 2000" is designed to provide technology and information to Meridian account managers who, freed of many of their former rigors of paperwork and other record-keeping chores, can more effectively concentrate on bringing value to their customers.

The bank doesn't just dump the new technological toys in the laps of its employees and expect them to be more efficient and deliver better customer service. They're trained not only on how to use the new tools but also on the new products they'll be able to sell in the new distributed computing environment. "It's getting more complex and that's why training and cross-training is so important," says McCullough.

Meridian's technology investment is just beginning to bear fruit, says Perrotty. "We're beginning to see the relationship with customers lengthen. We recognize the annuity value of a lifetime customer and that's done by making the relationship with a customer so convenient that they don't want to leave.

"I've been told that Merdian has the clearest strategy in the marketplace, which is that we'll make it easy for customers to do business with us whether it's at a branch, over the phone, through a personal computer at home or through a personal computer at the customer's business."

The Big Advantage of Smallness

Perhaps the biggest advantage of being the smallest regional player in the Pennsylvania banking arena is Meridian's size. "Being relatively small, we can move quickly. We're more like the Intrepid than the Queen Mary," says Perrotty, who adds that the simpler the strategy, the easier it is to execute.

"As we discover how people actually do their banking and understand their preferences, we can do a better job of tailoring our services to their needs. It's helping us to make the customer feel more important."

About 40 percent of Meridian's installment loans, for example, are transacted over the phone. Technology has helped Meridian reduce the time it takes to process a loan from 35 to 40 days to about eight to ten days.

Technology is also helping Meridian realize what it calls "relationship segmentation," in which the bank can deliver individualized services to identifiable groups. They include:

- Women business owners
- Latinos
- Senior citizens
- Baby boomers

Meridian has taken several other steps to outmarket the leading banks in its region, including:

■ **Maintaining a focus on the middle market.** Meridian does not turn up its nose at commercial loans as small as $200,000, says McCullough. "We'll do business with customers the big banks aren't interested in."

McCullough defines the middle market as companies, mostly private, with annual sales of $5 million up to $200 million. Meridian, he notes, concentrates on the lower end of that market. "Most of the banks around here say they are middle-market lenders, but their definition is very different from ours. They see the middle market as publicly held companies with $500 million to $1 billion in sales.

"In most cases, small businesses are the much more powerful group in terms of numbers and profit potential, because no one around here has figured out how to tap the market. That's why we're willing to fight for this market. We'll leave things like global cash management to PNC. Our success is a matter of sticking to the things that built us and not trying to be a J.P. Morgan or a Citicorp. That would be an exercise in futility."

At least until nationwide interstate banking comes to fruition, Meridian, he says, will reinforce its claim as a relationship banker by focusing its lending in its three-state region of Pennsylvania,

Delaware and New Jersey. "We live where our customers live and when we make a productive loan inside our region to build a plant or buy equipment then we create additional banking opportunities."

Meridian cuts loans to smaller companies in hope they will become large companies, which in turn will have larger credit demands, adds McCullough. About 95 percent of its loans are transacted in the bank's three-state region.

Meridian's middle-market positioning was articulated in a testimonial-style ad that features the photo of Fred Greenspoon, president of Garment Services Inc. The headline tersely states: "Tuesday. 11:59 a.m. The $2 million problem."

The text states: "I'll never forget it. Right before lunch on Tuesday I get this call. A client wants me to fill a $2 million T-shirt order. And it means going way beyond what my formula for credit would allow. So I get ahold of Angie at Meridian.

"She realized how big an opportunity this was for me. She worked with me. And she figured out a way to make it happen.

"You know in six years I had only three clients. No bank would even talk to me. But Meridian sat down with me, kept an open mind, and always looked ahead.

"Now, I have lots of clients, and lots of banks want to talk to me. But I'd rather talk to Angie."

By serving businesses in its own backyard, Perrotty says, Meridian can deliver all the pieces called for in a relationship banking model. "The big banks just want the lending piece of the relationship. They're not in a position to provide asset management, an investment service or a retirement program for a company's employees, because their corporate strategy is to do business at a higher tier.

"We're not going to confuse the market by saying we'll do loans down to $200,000, but won't do anything else like a pension program because the company is too small," says Perrotty.

■ **Branding its banking products.** Under the "Meridian Advantage" umbrella, the bank has developed a number of convenience-oriented products such as the "Advantage Phone Center," which offers seven-day-a-week, round-the-clock banking services; "Business Advantage," which allows businesses to conduct transactions over a PC; and the "Advantage Card," a debit card carried by about 428,000 people in the three-state region.

Consumers like the card, because it eliminates the need to carry a checkbook or large amounts of cash. It is especially popular with credit-averse customers such as senior citizens.

■ **Creating a sales and marketing culture rather than a banking culture.** "I joined this bank in 1975 when there was not even a semblance of a sales culture. People came to us, we didn't go to them," says McCullough. That all began to change with banking deregulation and the passage of limited, reciprocal interstate banking laws in the 1980's.

Meridian restructured its compensation system to reward its "relationship managers" (formerly known as commercial lenders) for achieving clearly defined sales goals. "We made it very explicit that they are no longer bankers but sales people."

Meridian has taken the very unbankerly tack of throwing a sales pep rally for about 3,000 of its employees in a college gymnasium. McCullough and recently retired bank president Ezekiel S. Ketchum were wheeled into the gym on a chariot and wore gladiators' helmets.

"They were throwing things and squirting green goo at us," recalls McCullough of his very fired-up troops. McCullough sent a clear signal that it's no longer business as usual at Meridian. Lending committees are a thing of the past. Authority now lies with individual relationship managers.

"We got deadly serious about sales and marketing. We had to create a new culture, because we knew what we were up against. We changed our thinking from being order takers to proactive initiators," says Perrotty.

Merdian's efforts to create intimate relations with its commercial and retail customers through new technology and a new culture, brings it almost full circle to the days when it was known as Berks County Trust. In 1952, it had four branches in Reading and assets of $84 million.

High-Tech and a Light Touch

Despite the banking company's rapid growth over the years, Meridian has never lost sight of its small-town bank characteristics. McCullough says Meridian's small-town touch combined with the development of financial services tailored to each market's needs have allowed it to succeed in markets as diverse as Philadelphia, the coal-mining country in Pennsylvania, and Amish farming communities like Paradise, Pennsylvania, where the bank has hitching posts for horse-drawn buggies.

"Meridian Bank has grown by staying home," says McCullough, who vows to perfect the use of high-tech and low-tech services to enhance the relationship with customers.

"We'll stick to what we do best, which is knowing who our customers are, what they need and when they want it. We'll never try to compete at a level we can't. We'll stay focused on what we're best at doing."

ALLEN-EDMONDS SHOE CORPORATION

NBC has described Allen-Edmonds as "the shoemaker to the stars." *The Washington Post* has described Allen-Edmonds as "the shoe of choice on Capitol Hill."

Why has the smart set elected to put its best foot forward in a pair of pricey Allen-Edmonds? As another famous shoemaker once said: "It's gotta be the shoes."

Allen-Edmonds dress shoes, meticulously handcrafted in the small Wisconsin community of Port Washington, have an almost cult-like following, but it takes more than the gloss of slick advertising to develop that sense of panache. It takes an almost perfect product. Allen-Edmonds' uncompromising commitment to producing a quality shoe has let it stand out in a field of much larger dress and casual shoemakers.

A Passion for Perfection

Overseeing Allen-Edmonds' quest for perfection is its colorful president, John Stollenwerk, who enthusiastically snaps up a shoe from the wall-sized display case in his office to highlight some of the finer points of the shoe's construction.

"As soon as you put on one of our shoes, you know if it fits or not. You don't wear the shoe around for a day or two. There's no breaking in one of our shoes." Stollenwerk headed an investment group that in 1980 bought Allen-Edmonds, a company founded in 1922 that had fallen on hard times.

One of his first tasks was to turn the foundering shoemaker into a marketing-driven operation that had a clear sense of who was or who should be wearing its product. "My second goal was for Allen-Edmonds to become the finest maker of men's dress shoes in the world."

"We are the only shoe company in the world without a metal shank and a 360-degree welt. (The welt is the leather piece that binds the upper, insole and outsole together). Our product conforms to the shape of your foot, rather than your foot conforming to the shoe."

Outlasting the Average Car

Allen-Edmonds shoes are designed to outlast a person's car. Each shoe goes through 212 steps before it leaves the factory with a price-tag ranging from $150 up to $1,500 for those who like the feel of alligator on their toes. At the factory, the leather is carefully scrutinized for any sign of imperfection.

During the cutting process, artisans with years of practice cut a pair of shoes from the same skin so there is no variation in the appearance, feel or fit of the shoe.

It's no wonder the shoes have found their way onto the feet of such luminaries as Bill Clinton, George Bush, Phil Graham, Ted Koppel, Clint Eastwood and Danny DeVito. The shoes are for men only. Allen-Edmonds discontinued its line of women's shoes in 1993 to launch a line of mens' casual shoes called Lifestyles.

No Fear of Retaliation

When Allen-Edmonds trotted out its new line of casual shoes in 1993, Stollenwerk says he was not concerned about triggering retaliatory reactions from shoemakers like Timberland or Wolverine, which produce a more rugged style of casual shoe. "Our Lifestyles are not performance shoes and our price points are higher."

Confronting the outdoor shoemakers head-on would be foolish. "First of all, we're a small player in that market. As a private company, there was no reason to go that route. It would be stupid on our part. It's like kicking an elephant to see if it will move. Obviously, it can return the kick with a lot more force," says Stollenwerk. "What sets us apart is the comfort of our shoes and the range of sizes and widths. The competition can't match us there."

Allen-Edmonds takes several steps to communicate its craftsmanship, including:

■ **Conveying a distinct sense of quality in each ad, catalog and newsletter.** Allen-Edmonds' product literature has a rich, understated look to it. "Our brochures and booklets go into great detail about the steps we take to produce a quality shoe," says Stollenwerk. Nicely photographed in four colors, the shoes get heroic treatment on each page.

Allen-Edmonds spends about $3 million a year to create ads that target businessmen and professionals who read such publications as *The Wall Street Journal, GQ, Fortune* or *Forbes.* "We do quasi third-party endorsements that say such things as: 'To lawyers the evidence of natural materials is indisputable' or 'Surgeons admire flawless stitching like this.'"

Allen-Edmonds has also run print ads featuring a cut-away illustration of one of its shoes highlighting the calfskin upper, the leather insole and other product features. The ad reinforces Allen-Edmonds' use of all-natural materials. The company also runs occasional spots on network and cable television.

■ **Motivating shoe retailers to push its product.** "Ours is a product that has to be sold rather than bought because of the higher price points," says Stollenwerk. "It just can't sit there on the racks with everybody else." Stollenwerk has personally visited hundreds of retailers around the world that carry the Allen-Edmonds brand to light a fire under them.

"I want the retailers telling the customers what we stand for and that Allen-Edmonds is the best shoe in the world." One incentive program to get sales reps to push Allen-Edmonds shoes rewarded the top seller with an all-expense paid trip to Port Washington, population 8,612. The trip also includes a guided tour of the Allen-Edmonds factory where the sales rep can gain an even greater appreciation for what goes into the shoe.

"We rely heavily on the retailer to tell our story to the consumer," he adds. Allen-Edmonds operates 17 of its own shoe stores in the U.S. and Europe. Stollenwerk foresees no expansion of its own chain of stores because of high overhead costs.

■ **Publicity.** To further Allen-Edmonds' almost legendary status, the company works with costumers on feature films, television shows and Broadway plays. Retailers tip off the company when a celebrity buys a pair of its shoes. The news finds its way to Allen-Edmonds' semi-annual magazine, *Shoe Wrap*.

The celebrities don't seem to mind. In fact, actor Ernest Borgnine makes it a point to drop by Allen-Edmonds each summer. Actor Brian Dennehy called Allen-Edmonds directly to request a pair of white bucks for a scene in an ABC television pilot being filmed in Canada.

Allen-Edmonds got wind that Bill Clinton pads around the Oval Office in Allen-Edmonds shoes from an Arkansas retailer who began selling to him while he was governor.

The Hollywood Mystique

Virginia Riddle, the company's director of public relations, says the publicity on celebrity shoeing is worth its weight in gold.

The company makes shoes in 164 different sizes, from 5 to 18, and widths from AAAA to EEE. Allen-Edmonds can also custom design a shoe for the hard-to-fit types like Brad Millard, a Seattle teenager who stands 7 feet, 3 inches tall and weighs 300 pounds. He desperately wanted a pair of dress shoes but no store—not even Nordstrom—carried his size: 24 EEEEEE. Nordstrom, one of Allen-Edmonds' leading retailers, called Port Washington for some help.

Allen-Edmonds designers, who requested measurements, photos and a cast of Millard's imposing feet, were able to accommodate the youngster. The story was national news, which didn't cost Allen-Edmonds a penny.

Keeping a High Profile

Stollenwerk has been a newsmaker in his own right, especially after kicking up his heels over shabby treatment from foreign bureaucrats who've slapped absurdly high tariffs on his shoes. He appeared on ABC's "Good Morning America," on NBC's "Today Show," and has been interviewed for *Business Week*, *Newsweek* and trade publications.

Stollenwerk caused a stir in 1987 when he crashed the Tokyo Shoe Fair. "The Japanese Shoe Association was trying to keep me from displaying samples of our products. I was really steamed, because I had an invitation through a representative of the European Economic Community," he says.

"I told them I would stand in front of the door with my sample cases until they let me in. To save face, they set up a little booth for me in the lobby." Despite his bold stand, Allen-Edmonds isn't making much progress penetrating the Japanese market, which Stollenwerk maintains is terribly protectionist.

Penetrating Japan

The company, which makes 350,000 pairs of shoes a year, only sold 1,000 pairs in 1994 in Japan, where tariffs raise the price of the shoes to as much as $500. About 15 percent of the company's $55 million in 1994 sales was international. "I'd like to see it closer to 25 percent, because there are only so many people in the United States who will buy our product at our price."

Italy and Germany have been Allen-Edmonds' most vibrant foreign markets where it's selling about 20,000 pairs of shoes a year. Sales are growing in France and Spain, and throughout Asia.

Regardless of what country the consumer calls home, Allen-Edmonds wants to keep him forever. "We have a five-person staff whose job is to satisfy and retain customers," says Stollenwerk, who personally answers letters directed to him from people who weren't completely satisfied with a product.

Pleasing the Customer

"I get on the phone and hear them out. Then I send them a brass shoe horn in a velvet pouch as a follow-up gesture," says Stollenwerk. "I was in the office early one day and called a guy in Salt Lake City who had written me a letter. I got him out of bed, because I forgot about the time change. I told him I was really sorry."

Continuing, he says: "The customer is paramount. A lot of companies have forgotten that. They view customers as a necessary evil. Nobody wins in a love-hate relationship."

Another tack that Allen-Edmonds takes to keep its customers is its recrafting service. Unique among shoemakers, the repair and rejuvenation service brings older Allen-Edmonds shoes back to life through the same processes used in their original construction.

Stollenwerk isn't concerned that the recrafting service, for which the company charges $80, cannibalizes future sales. He figures the loyalty it engenders among customers outweighs the cost.

By insisting on perfection in the product development and continued creative marketing of the shoes and the company's image, Stollenwerk says Allen-Edmonds is only now hitting its stride. "It starts with quality suppliers and quality retailers and ends with customers who are crazy about shoes."

6 The Shadow Casters

Sometimes, "share of mind" is better than share of market. That's especially true in a company's early going. Ask any underdog marketer how tough it is to be taken seriously in those perilous days after first hanging out the shingle.

Savvy underdogs manage to cast a shadow on the market that makes them seem bigger than they actually are. Be it pluck or puffery, this outmarketing tactic has worked marvelously for companies who have gone on to become leaders in their field.

Devon Direct Marketing and Advertising tried for months to get its foot in the door at MCI. Finally, one of its well-polished direct mail pieces found its mark. An MCI executive sorting through his mail at 6 a.m. one day jarred Devon Direct's Ron Greene from his sleep to ask him why his fledgling agency should handle MCI's direct response advertising.

Although only half awake in the bedroom of his home where Devon Direct was then housed, Greene must have sounded convincing. In the next two years, Devon Direct would produce and send a staggering 150 million pieces of direct mail on MCI's behalf. The battle with AT&T was engaged and tiny Devon Direct was on the map.

Thrifty Car Rental was suffering from a 'mom-and-pop' look at its nationwide chain of rental outlets. One of the first things a new management team did was give Thrifty a big company look. From the uniforms its employees wore to the ads broadcast on network TV, Thrifty emulated the look and feel of the industry's big dogs like Hertz and Avis.

Although substantially smaller than the industry leaders, Thrifty's shadow-casting strategy paid off, as leisure and business travelers elevated the underdog to one of their leading choices. Once Thrifty projected itself onto the same playing field as the big dogs, it began to differentiate itself. But first things first.

Talk radio has been a largely boy's-night-out-affair. Then along came Debbie Nigro, who's landed her "Working Mom on the Run" syndicated talk show on some 150 stations nationwide, including several of the nation's Top Ten markets.

On a shoe-string budget, Nigro and business partner Jeff Troncone worked tirelessly to personally convince station managers and sponsors that their show was worthy of the big-time. "We always made the program seem much bigger than it actually was in the early days," says Troncone. "I made Debbie seem like she was 10 feet tall."

Stratco, a struggling supplier to refineries, realized it had to break out of its long-running slump if it hoped to survive. But only the boldest of strokes would help to recast it as a petroleum and chemical engineering consulting firm.

Going for broke, Stratco sponsored a three-day seminar on a technology in which had developed a strong expertise. Stratco's new president Diane Graham invited the leading executives and engineers in the petroleum industry. And guess what? They showed up—114 of them. Impressed by Stratco's orchestration of the conference and its deft display of its expertise, the leading oil companies began tapping Stratco for its consulting services. A little bravado goes a long way.

Now, meet the Shadow Casters.

DEVON DIRECT MARKETING & ADVERTISING

The brightest moment of Devon Direct Marketing and Advertising's early days came in the predawn darkness when the ring of a telephone broke the stillness in the bedroom of Ron Greene's Philadelphia home. It was MCI calling.

MCI wasn't calling at that ungodly hour to pitch a new residential long-distance calling program to the Greenes. It was much better than that.

MCI wanted Greene to hustle down to its Washington, D.C., headquarters to tell them why Devon Direct should become its first-ever direct response advertising agency. MCI wanted Greene there the next morning.

Frothing at the Bit

At that time, Devon Direct had less than $1 million in billings, two employees and an office being run out of Greene's home. But it was frothing at the bit to pitch MCI, the telecommunications upstart girding for an historic marketing battle with giant AT&T. Underdogs apparently have a soft spot for their fellow underdogs—except MCI had little idea how much of an underdog Devon Direct really was.

"I certainly didn't want them to know I was running this business out of my home. In those days, it sent the wrong signals," says Greene, managing principal of the agency that today employs 130 and bills about $140 million a year. The business is no longer run out of Greene's home, but in an office building in the Philadelphia suburb of Berwyn where Devon Direct tends to a roster of blue-chip clients like Nutri/System, ADT, financial services provider Advanta Corporation, PrimeStar (a direct-broadcast satellite company), and IBM Recovery Services.

"The prevailing notion in those days was: 'How could someone working from their home ever provide effective services for a major corporation?' "

The Art of Looming Large

Devon Direct was able to cast a large enough shadow to convince MCI that it was a player, and one that could help take customers away from AT&T. Devon Direct's breakthrough took place, however, only after a series of rejections from MCI.

Greene had been sending MCI well-designed direct mail pieces touting not only the agency's capabilities but the virtues of direct response advertising. Unlike long-term, brand-building general advertising, direct response is intended to elicit an immediate reaction from a reader. Direct response, unlike general advertising, is much more measurable.

Devon Direct's Wake-Up Call

All his appeals to MCI had either been rejected or ignored. "I remember telling my wife: 'How can these guys not talk to me? This is a done deal if they only let me in the door.' But then I figured they're big business. They are never going to talk to a little guy."

That was until Ed Carter, who at the time was MCI's executive vice president in charge of marketing and advertising, picked up the telephone in his office shortly after 6 a.m. and jarred Greene from his sleep. "Carter is at work re-reading my letter and he decides he wants to talk to me and he wants to talk to me right now! It must have never occurred to him that someone else was not at his desk."

But Greene wasn't complaining. He was in D.C. the next morning to make the presentation of a lifetime. Here's Greene's advice on how underdogs can win business from a big client.

■ **Get their attention.** Devon Direct used well-polished direct mail to win an audience with MCI. Even though Greene's fledgling business was tiny, he made sure that it communicated a big company look.

The mailings conveyed one succinct idea: that direct response advertising will work because it speaks individually to a customer or prospect. "It's powerful," says Greene.

■ **Educate your client.** "Although MCI was not considering bringing direct mail into their overall advertising mix, we were able to convince them otherwise once we got our foot in the door," says Greene. "I sold them on the idea that they really could take control of their advertising results.

"I told MCI that they could either match or lower the acquisition cost they were experiencing from other channels like telemarketing or television. They'd also be able to track the response."

■ **Demonstrate that your service is a more cost efficient.** While talking to MCI about its advertising strategy, discussion turned to some collateral pieces that MCI was mailing to help motivate its sales reps who served the company's business customers.

"I saw the stuff and learned that MCI was paying about $3 per package. I asked MCI if they would like to do the same thing for 30 cents per package." Naturally, MCI was interested, but could Devon Direct deliver?

"I found a way to do the project at the cost I promised," says Greene. "The moon, the stars and the sun were in alignment, because if I was going up against a print-oriented, direct-response advertising agency for that business, there was no way I could have offered to do it for a tenth of the cost."

The agency that was producing the packages had expertise in producing television commercials but not print. MCI began to realize it was paying way too much for its print packages.

Had there been another direct response agency under consideration, Greene suspects he would have only been given the chance to prove that his work was more creative and higher quality. The money MCI saved by tapping Devon Direct to do the print packages was used to defray the costs of the direct-response test aimed at consumers.

The successful test run of a consumer-targeted direct response ad campaign was the first of more than 150 million pieces of direct mail Devon Direct would produce for MCI over the next two years. Today, Devon Direct is MCI's principal direct response advertising agency.

■ **Tell the world who your clients are.** After landing a client, particularly a blue-chip company, Greene says underdogs should let prospective clients know who they are doing work for. It helps build credibility and will not drive prospective clients away "thinking that you're too busy for them. That was one of the early mistakes I made in starting this business."

Racing Against the Clock

MCI, Greene suspects, was willing to entrust a small, unheard-of agency with its direct response work because "they were in a race against the clock. I think they were willing to consider anything reasonable at that point." A 1984 federal court ruling struck down AT&T's long-distance phone service monopoly and opened the flood gates to new competition.

MCI wanted to get there first. It took a big step in that direction when Devon Direct launched a first-of-its-kind neighborhood-by-neighborhood direct marketing campaign that convinced hundreds of thousands of AT&T customers to switch to MCI. It was one of Devon Direct's earliest examples of pushing beyond traditional direct marketing.

Direct mail, with its ability to pinpoint a target, was the perfect advertising vehicle for the type of campaign MCI had in mind to spoil AT&T's party. "Let's say my neighborhood had Dial 1 service (or access to an alternative long-distance carrier) but only on my side of the street. I could mail an MCI package to a particular person that I knew would go Dial 1 on a specific date.

"We were able to marry telephone numbers to zip codes to reach the consumer who was about to be offered the choice of a new service. We reached specific members of a target audience much more efficiently than print or television advertising."

Complementing Madison Avenue

Devon Direct doesn't consider itself a competitor of Madison Avenue, which is best known for producing splashy, image-oriented print and television advertising campaigns. "There is a real role for general advertising because it builds brand awareness. General and direct are two essential elements to maximize the impact of a campaign. Direct mail will create a new link to the customer and strengthen the general advertising component with a targeted message."

Greene says Devon Direct has a distinct advantage over general agencies because the agency can usually execute a campaign for less money but with more creativity and higher impact. Devon Direct, he says, can also outgun the Madison Avenue agencies' direct response boutiques.

Greene was no stranger to the science of direct response advertising. For the seven years before launching Devon Direct in 1983, Greene was vice president of advertising and marketing at the Franklin Mint in Philadelphia. He was one of the driving forces behind the Mint's transformation from a coin minting operation into one of the nation's leading direct marketers of collectibles.

Dropping the Plates

He and Jim Perry, the Mint's vice president of product development, joined forces to launch their own shop to direct market porcelain plates and hand-painted sculptures. Perry has since retired from the agency.

Greene and Perry never did much marketing of plates or sculptures, because, after launching Devon Direct, they found they were frequently approached by businesses asking them to share their tips and techniques on direct marketing. Sensing a more lucrative opportunity, Devon Direct began recasting itself as a direct response advertising agency.

Landing the MCI account put Devon Direct on the map. The

fledgling agency was then able to parlay the expertise it was developing with MCI into other telecommunications accounts like McCaw Cellular, which today is a unit of AT&T.

Generating 12 Million Calls

When Ed Carter switched from MCI to a similar marketing role at smaller rival Sprint Corporation, he invited Devon Direct to come along. Devon Direct resigned its MCI account and began developing breakthrough direct marketing ideas for Sprint, including the Foncard, a flashy, silver mylar credit card that helped Sprint generate 12 million additional calls a year.

Devon Direct put the cards directly in the hands of business travelers by placing them on the ticket jackets of the major airlines. Devon Direct later returned to MCI.

Although Devon Direct has grown to become the nation's second-largest independent direct-response agency, it continues to think like an underdog. "We haven't changed that much," says Greene, whose memory of the agency's scrappy, go-for-broke days is still fresh.

The Power of Customer Information

"Something we did right from the start was to show the companies we worked with the value of the information they were sitting on with their existing customers. We told them that if they could take that information and understand the buying habits of their customers, they could convert that into a continuing source of revenue. They could build a long-term relationship with that customer."

Retention or relationship marketing is a hot subject these days, but Devon Direct has been doing it for MCI and other clients since 1983. "The general advertising agencies weren't focused on retaining customers but acquiring new ones. They ignored the relationships.

"But companies and their agencies are finally discovering that they spend an enormous amount of money to acquire customers, but for a few dollars more they can also keep the ones they already have," says Greene.

Advances in database technology are making it easier to develop sophisticated profiles of customers. It's a technology that Devon Direct was quick to embrace.

Devon Direct practices what it preaches. In 1994, nearly 30 percent of its growth was generated from increased programs for existing clients.

Keeping the Customer

For MCI, Devon Direct developed an array of customer communication packages to reduce churn. Some direct mail packages simply thanked customers for their business or helped them better understand their bills; others offered customer service or alerted them to new services.

With an innovative use of personalization and calling data, Devon Direct showed MCI customers—in writing—the amount of money they could save by adding numbers to their "Friends and Family" calling circles.

It's Either Yes or No

In a campaign that won every major direct marketing award, Devon Direct mailed Bell Atlantic customers a brown paper bag that listed the 10 reasons to "bag your answering machine" and get "Answer Call," a voice messaging service. Customers were then instructed to toss their old answering machines in the bag for storage or disposal.

The "brown bag" campaign produced a response rate 50 percent higher than Bell Atlantic's traditional direct marketing programs by using the classic direct response technique of boiling down a consumer's decision-making process to a simple "yes" or "no."

"Instead of frustrating the consumer with a multiplicity of decisions, you reduce it to: 'Yes, I will buy or no, I will not.'" Presenting the customer or prospect with a simple proposition to buy or not to buy is only half the battle, however.

The proposition has to be creatively presented and packaged, according to Greene. "That's why we are able to compete against the big general agencies. We can bring some fresh thinking to the table. Clients, these days, are looking for strategies to maximize their communications. In the final analysis, you need to have great ideas."

In Devon Direct's early days, Greene says it was critical to "talk the walk," that is take on a big look to convince the big companies it was targeting that it could do big-time work. "We proved we could do it and that built our credibility in a hurry. Our challenge today is to keep 'walking the walk.'"

THRIFTY CAR RENTAL

An underdog that wants to be heard in the intensely competitive car rental industry needs a bark worse than its bite. Thrifty Car Rental barks with the big dogs by taking on the look and the feel of industry leaders Hertz and Avis, which are several times Thrifty's size.

"From an advertising point of view, we always try to look bigger than we are," says Bob Dimmick, vice president of marketing at Tulsa, Oklahoma-based Thrifty. "We like to look like one of the big guys."

Looking Like a Big Dog

By looking like one of the big guys—or big dogs—Thrifty puts itself on the same playing field as its larger rivals. Come decision time, explains Dimmick, Thrifty enjoys nearly the same top-of-mind awareness among leisure and business travelers as the industry leaders which substantially outspend Thrifty on the advertising front.

Avis, the No. 2 car rental company that's staked its claim to fame on the fact that "we try harder," spent an estimated $14 million on advertising in 1994. Thrifty, by comparison, could muster only about half that amount, according to Dimmick. (Advertising tracking services base their estimates on the 'reported' cost of a single ad page in a magazine or a standard block of air time on a television station.)

Through prudent media buying and sponsorship of leading sporting events, Dimmick says the $7 million in 'reported' ad spending had the actual impact of about $11 million. "We try to make every dollar we spend on advertising look like 10," says Dimmick. "The name of the company is Thrifty, not stupid," he says with a laugh. "We have to seek out every advantage we can."

Seizing New Opportunities

Leveraging every marketing opportunity possible is how Thrifty casts a big shadow on the $12.5 billion car rental business, says Meloyde Blancett-Scott, Thrifty's staff vice president of corporate communications and planning. Thrifty, which has more than 1,000 rental centers worldwide, is a unit of Chrysler Corporation, which supplies Thrifty its vehicles.

Because Thrifty can't match the advertising budget of the Big 2, it strives to make the most of its word-of-mouth marketing opportunities. Word-of-mouth costs nothing, yet carries more weight in the marketplace, notes Blancett-Scott.

"We leverage the relationship with our employees, because they're the ones who touch the customers on a daily basis and create these positive experiences that are then transmitted by satisfied customers through word-of-mouth to prospective customers."

Partnering With Customers

"If you can leverage that relationship with your employees so that they in turn create a partnership with the customers, you'll be more successful in competing against larger competitors. We don't forget our employees. We recognize how important they are in our marketing."

Thrifty takes other key steps to create the impression that they are as big and as good as the bigger car rental companies, including:

■ **Creating a big company look.** In its earlier days, the company was "a menagerie of mom and pop operations with no consistent look," says Blancett-Scott.

"We decided to look just like the big guys. If they have impressive-looking signage, then we have impressive-looking signage; if they have nice looking counters with computers, then we'll have the same; and if their people wear crisp-looking uniforms, then our people will have crisp-looking uniforms. The strategy worked, because we were then perceived as a major car rental company," she says.

■ **Sponsoring sporting events.** Thrifty is the title sponsor of the Holiday Bowl in San Diego. Sporsorship exposes the Thrifty name to football fans and serves as the basis of other marketing programs such as Holiday Bowl Sweepstakes and a Holiday Bowl party for franchisees, as well. Sponsorship of the event also includes a commitment to buy media during the game.

Thrifty is the official rental car company of the U.S. Figure Skating Association and it sponsors one of the tour events. Thrifty is also the official car rental company of the Champions Senior U.S. Tennis Tour and is the official rental car company of the Six Flags Amusement Parks.

"We make tickets available to our franchisees and their employees. The sponsorships and events help boost our advertising dollars and strengthen our corporate and local personality," says Dimmick. Franchisees appreciate when Thrifty casts a big shadow on the marketplace, because it helps drive their car rentals.

Franchisees contribute a small percentage of their revenues to help defray both national and local advertising expenses. An advertising committee of franchisees approves advertising budgets and plans.

"We went from a cable TV advertiser to an almost exclusively network TV advertiser," says Dimmick. "We advertise on such programs as Good Morning America, the Super Bowl, the Winter Olympics, college football and prime time programming. It has built top-of-mind awareness and made us a leading choice among people renting cars for leisure or business. It has also made our franchisees and their employees proud to be a part of Thrifty."

Setting Itself Apart

Having taken on the appearance of a major car rental company, the next step was to differentiate Thrifty from the likes of Hertz and Avis. Rather than try to slug it out with the big companies at airport rental locations where business people were the prime target, Thrifty positioned itself as "Your neighborhood Thrifty car rental." Its advertising plays up the Thrifty's off-airport locations and its low prices.

Although 70 percent of all car rentals are from airport locations, the suburban marketplace was growing faster than the business traveler market, according to Dimmick. "Our mix between airport and off-airport rentals is now about 50/50." Thrifty has gone aggressively after the leisure/insurance replacement market in the suburbs with an emphasis on the leisure market. "It's a level playing field for us in the neighborhood centers. The price competition at the airports is very cutthroat," says Dimmick.

"The insurance replacement market, where motorists rent a car while theirs is in the repair shop, is only a small portion of our business. That is dominated by Enterprise and Snappy, which operate cars much longer than the traditional car rental companies. They'll keep a car for two or three years and put a lot of miles on them. At our neighborhood and airport sites, we have the latest Chrysler models available," says Dimmick.

Tapping a Wealth of Opportunities

To help increase Thrifty's neighborhood business, the marketing department prepared a list of 200 reasons why people should rent from Thrifty.

The list explains to franchisees how they can exploit local opportunities by advertising in Chamber of Commerce bulletins or by providing special programs for members of churches or discount programs to holders of certain bank cards.

The list provides marketing tips on how to target local institutions. For example, Thrifty recommends its franchisees use direct mail to offer special discounts to members of private clubs and country clubs. Florists are told about the franchisee's fleet for possible use during such high-volume periods as Valentine's Day, Secretary's Day or Mother's Day.

A second list provides 228 additional ways to rent cars. Potential customers range from advertising salespeople to zoos. A growing number of Thrifty's neighborhood customers are renting a minivan for a long weekend or a week's vacation. The family car often isn't big enough for special events.

Always a Reason to Rent

"People like to rent a big car or a convertible to go to high school or family reunions, funerals, graduations, proms, anniversaries or Valentine's Day. There's always a reason for renting a car in a local marketplace," says Dimmick, who notes that average Thrifty rental is 4.2 days versus the industry average of 2.6 days.

"We measure everything by time and mileage—how long the customers kept the car and how much they paid for the entire rental. Our time and mileage in our neighborhood markets has been growing phenomenally. Revenue in 1994 was up 18 percent over 1993," says Dimmick. Thrifty's total world-wide rental revenues in 1994 were $452 million.

Another growing stream of revenue are people who, rather than test drive a car from an auto dealer, will rent a Chrysler vehicle from Thrifty. "They take it for a few days or a week to see if it's really the car for them. They learn a lot more about the vehicle than they can on a quick test drive," he says. "People are smart. They don't want to go through buyer's remorse."

Thrifty takes several other steps to help it outmarket the leaders in the car rental industry, including:

■ **Showing the customers a good time.** "In the car rental business, the relationship between the employee and customer is pretty intense," says Blancett-Scott. "People are running late for a meeting or a flight. It's not the best situation. But in the neighborhood market you have a little more time to develop a relationship with the customer. It's not rush, rush, rush like at the airport."

Blancett-Scott who carries the second title of "staff vice president for reputation, spirit and planning" has created a series of what she calls "enthusiasm days" at Thrifty outlets. For example, on Valentine's Day, Thrifty customers can win a small prize by correctly answering questions posed in a "Great Lovers Through History Quiz."

"The day's general theme is that Thrifty loves its customers. It's all designed so that we're perceived as the kind of company people want to do business with," says Blancett-Scott.

■ **Motivating employees to show customers a good time.** "We believe that if you don't have happy employees you won't have happy customers. That's the bottom line," says Blancett-Scott. "We're fooling ourselves if we think we can achieve a high degree of customer satisfaction without focusing on employee happiness. That's the primary way of achieving customer satisfaction. Employees who embrace our philosophy carry it forward with their customers."

Thrifty's franchisees and their employees have adopted the principles of "positively outrageous service" established by business consultant T. Scott Gross, author of the *Positively Outrageous Service* books. "We try to add a little spice to the life of our employees. These events create an opportunity for exchange and conversation an employee would not normally have with a customer in a routine work day.

"By becoming employee-centered, we increase our word-of-mouth awareness with customers who have been treated with greater fairness and enthusiasm. It translates into the ability to ask for higher prices because of the added value of higher perceived customer satisfaction."

Quality customer service is what sets one company apart from another. "The car rental business has become a commodity product. Customers have been known to change their loyalties for as little as a dollar a day," says Blancett-Scott.

"We try to differentiate ourselves on the basis of not only a quality car but a high level of service. People get a feeling for our personality and want to come back. We want employees to take such good care of the customer that the customer wouldn't possibly think of going anywhere else to rent a car. We create the strong impression that we are this neighborly car rental company."

Motivated employees are more likely to take extraordinary customer service measures such as driving a customer from Miami down to the Florida Keys after the woman forgot to pack her driver's license.

■ **Involving franchisees in the local community.** To cement its bonds with the local community, Thrifty franchise operators and their employees are encouraged to get involved in their neighborhood. "We like them to get involved with community institutions and meet the members. It's a big part of our neighborhood philosophy," says Dimmick.

New franchisees get a sense for what's expected of them and a sense for Thrifty's culture by spending a week at Thrifty's headquarters where they attend seminars and training sessions, and meet with the company's top executives.

■ **Hiring the right people.** "There are certain personality types who should not be in a high customer contact position," says Blancett-Scott. "We are developing a structured program that will serve as a template for other franchise owners on how to hire the right people and then train them so that they can make the most of their customer contact abilities. We want to put people and their energies together in a way that you can't bottle or buy."

■ **Creating new products.** Thrifty helped pioneer the use of automated kiosks for quick check-in and check-out. The Thrifty Automated Rental Center or TARC is often used in hotel lobbies or at corporate campuses where a particular company has an account.

"It's a way for us to take care of large corporate accounts without having to tie up personnel for 16 to 24 hours a day," says Dimmick.

All the marketing steps Thrifty has taken in recent years are designed to make the company look big but act small. "The best of both worlds," adds Dimmick.

SWEET TALK PRODUCTIONS

It takes more than sweet talk to develop one of the hottest nationally syndicated radio talk shows. Debbie Nigro, host of "Working Mom on the Run," has used dashes of bravado and entrepreneurial hustle to get her show on the air in some 150 cities.

A single mother and a former morning drive personality on a major New York City radio station, Nigro uses her own harried life as the basis of the weekly, three-hour radio talk show that has hit home with the nation's growing legion of working mothers.

"The show is a page torn right out of my life," says Nigro. Inspiration for the show, heard on Saturdays, arrived amid a particularly tumultuous time in her life. She had lost her radio program, gone through a divorce and was struggling to launch a new career in the international commodities business.

Strapped for Cash

"My phone bills to Paris were larger than anything I could ever hope to make in the business," says Nigro half-jokingly. Not so funny was the fact that Nigro was so strapped for cash that her car registration was cancelled, because she didn't have enough money to pay her parking tickets.

"I realized I was going off in a wildly ridiculous direction. I had to regroup. I told myself that I have to sit still and think about what I do best and what makes me happy."

Although she was so disgusted after losing her morning drive job that she refused to listen to the radio for nearly two years, Nigro came to the conclusion that radio was still her true love. If only she could package the agonies and ecstasies of a working mom on the run into a radio format.

Then along came Jeff Troncone, a former theatrical agent whose business had gone sour. Troncone saw Nigro on a cable television show she was hosting in Westchester County, New York. "I felt something through the screen and called her up," says Troncone.

Launching Sweet Talk

Love blossomed and so did a business partnership they call Sweet Talk Productions, which self-syndicates "Working Mom on the Run." Armed with a great idea, but lacking money, sponsors and stations, Nigro and Troncone decided to go for broke.

"When you have nothing to lose, you take the shot because anything that happens is good," says Troncone. Using the studio of a station where Nigro once worked, the pair produced a one-hour pilot for the program.

"Simultaneously, we made three copies of the program's highlights and gave them to a friend who knew some executives at Avon Products," says Troncone. With the little money Nigro and Troncone had left, they bought three Sony Walkmans, inserted the tape, gave it to their friend with the Avon connection and crossed their fingers.

Avon Responds Quickly

They didn't have to wait long. "We heard from Avon right away," says Troncone. "They liked what they heard on the tape so much that they called Debbie and asked for a meeting. What they heard on the tape was their life. It hit a raw nerve with them. Plus, the timing was perfect. Avon was looking to do something non-traditional with its advertising."

Avon, a $4 billion cosmetics company, threw its weight behind Sweet Talk in the form of a $3,000 check. "They told us to take the show national," says Troncone. Avon's backing of the program was worth far more than the $3,000 investment. "That $3,000 seemed like more than $300,000 at the time. It was an enormous step for us because Fortune 500 companies do not invest in media properties that can't give them national exposure. It was a lark on their part."

But it was an investment in which Avon realized an enormous return, because Nigro and Troncone pulled off the seemingly impossible mission of creating a nationally syndicated radio show with only $3,000 in seed money. Talk about an underdog challenge!

Reaching for a National Audience

Their quest began in 1993 with only two stations—one in Westchester County, the other in Greenwich, Connecticut. It was a far cry from the national syndication that Avon said should be the goal of the program.

Sweet Talk Productions took several key marketing steps, including:

■ **Talking big.** "We always made the program seem much bigger than it actually was in the early days," says Troncone. "I made Debbie seem like she was 10 feet tall. The key thing is that you have to not only know how to sell but have something to sell. In our case, Debbie was the product."

When station managers would ask Troncone how many other stations had committed to the program, Troncone would tell them that during the previous week two more stations had agreed to air the program.

That was true, although Sweet Talk was paying the new stations to run the program. "But I could tell Avon and other station managers that we were adding stations," says Troncone, who was always quick to add that Avon was a sponsor of the program. The backing of the Fortune 500 company with a household name helped open some doors during Sweet Talk's perilous early days.

Buying air time on new stations to build a network quickly burned through the $3,000 Avon had invested. The gamble paid off as more stations began to incorporate the show into their programming.

"Talking the big game can only get you so far, because you have to continually back it up with something credible. You can't just use bluster," he says. "That's why a lot of entrepreneurs fail. Their intentions are terrific, but you need an innate sense for when to pull and when to push."

■ **Build credibility through third-party endorsements.** Sweet Talk would "warm the doorknobs" of the station managers it was targeting by sending testimonial letters from other station managers who were pleased with the results the show was generating.

"I can't tell you how much our listeners enjoy your show," wrote Dan Flatt, operations manager of WCTC-AM in New Brunswick, New Jersey. "Every time I talk to a listener, I get the same response: 'I love the show because I can relate to it.' You have definitely hit on something here. I think people hear that your life is just like theirs and it's nice to know that they aren't alone."

Getting station managers to adopt "Working Mom" was a tough sell because the station has to drop another program to make way for a new one. Station managers, Troncone found, were impressed to read letters from their counterparts who took the step and reaped the benefits.

■ **Personally sell the show.** Even though the show now has tremendous momentum of its own, Nigro tries to go on as many sales calls to stations as possible. "We bend over backwards to make the show work for the station," says Nigro.

"Jeff and I go in person to meet the key people and introduce ourselves. We meet with the sales staff and give them ideas on how to make money on the show. Almost nobody does that."

In the early days of the show, Nigro also paid visits to the small sponsors. "I went to the hair salon or the local supermarket. It really made a difference in selling them on the show," she says. "Never pass up an opportunity to meet somebody and never be afraid to call anybody regardless of their position or their perceived power.

Put yourself on an even plane with them and have enough confidence in yourself to make the call."

■ **Create a product or program that is unique yet has broad appeal.** In developing and launching the program, Nigro says, "I kept hearing a common chord running through womens' lives with whomever I was talking to. It was that our lives are very busy and it's impossible to do everything perfectly. Women should not feel guilty. We need to laugh a little. My premise is that if you can make someone laugh and smile then you get their attention and give them additional information.

"We found a niche. It was something so obvious, yet no one else was doing it," Nigro adds. "Woman need information about their lives and increasingly about their businesses. Half the small businesses in America will be women-owned by the year 2000."

Her guests have included U.S. Secretary of Labor Robert Reich, New Jersey governor Christine Whitman and Judsen Culbreth, editor-in-chief of *Working Mother* magazine. With woman making up more than half the population, Nigro says she could never understand why there were so few female voices in talk radio. "I can bring a unique perspective to the airwaves."

■ **Don't take "no" for an answer.** It's basic, but it works, says Nigro. "Jeff has taught me that no doesn't necessarily mean no. It's often an invitation to do something or propose an idea a different way. We heard a lot of 'no's' in trying to sell this program. Most of them later became 'yes's'."

■ **Use publicity and public relations.** Because it carries more weight with people than advertising, Nigro says Sweet Talk has invested more in public relations. "When people read about you in a publication they take it at face value. It's important to let people know you exist, so you can become one of their choices."

Sweet Talk's press kit included articles on Nigro's show that appeared in *The Wall Street Journal, Chicago Tribune* and major trade publications.

Underdog Principles Pay Off

By 1995, Sweet Talk's application of several underdog marketing principles were paying dividends.

The program was on several of the nation's Top 10 markets, including Seattle, Detroit and Houston. National advertisers like Sears, Roebuck & Co., Toyota, Procter & Gamble Co.'s Folgers Coffee, and Little Caesar's had signed on as sponsors paying about $1,500 for a 30-second spot. Avon was a continuing sponsor. Listenership was approaching 1 million.

In March of 1995, Nigro began broadcasting a daily, two-minute vignette featuring items from *Working Mother* magazine. Sponsored by Avon, the vignettes are heard in about 250 markets. "Working Mom on the Run" is now broadcast from a leased ABC radio studio in New York.

More Selling Ahead

Sweet Talk is far from satisfied, says Troncone, who would like "Working Mom on the Run" heard in as many as 400 to 500 markets. Cracking that many markets will require persuading hundreds more station managers to sign on with the show.

That will require Sweet Talk to outmarket such radio syndication giants as Westwood One Entertainment, ABC and Talk America, which are among the eight or nine leading syndicators of radio programs. Rush Limbaugh's show, distributed by EFM Media, is heard in more than 600 markets.

"When you're going up against the big syndicators you have to keep all the balls in the air at once," says Troncone of the art of juggling the show's finances, production, content and advertising all at the same time.

Sweet, Not Caustic

Nigro doesn't go for the caustic fare that have made Limbaugh and shock jock Howard Stern so popular. "It's clean programming," says

Troncone. "A selling point with the stations is that they are not going to get sued for putting Debbie on the air."

"We manage to be successful without being obnoxious on the air or off the air," says Nigro. "Timing has a lot to do with our success. Women are much more visible in places where they have not been in the past, particularly the workplace. As a result, they need information, they need to commiserate and they need to know they are not alone. My show has given them a voice."

STRATCO INCORPORATED

It seemed like a pretentious idea for a small, struggling refinery equipment supplier to host a three-day petroleum engineering conference that would attract such oil industry heavyweights as Amoco, Chevron, Texaco and Unocal. But it worked.

"That seminar was the beginning of our new look," says Diane Graham, president of Stratco, Inc., which today is a prosperous $25 million chemical and process engineering firm based in Kansas City, Missouri.

None of the 114 engineers or other oil company executives who attended that conference in Houston in 1981, however, had much of an idea of how small Stratco really was.

Although the company was founded in 1928 and had developed a reputation in the petroleum industry for supplying top-notch equipment, tiny Stratco was clearly on the ropes. The number of employees at the company had fallen to only 12.

Three company presidents had died in a seven-year period between 1974 and 1981. "My dad died less than two years after buying controlling interest in the company. He was succeeded by my mother who died eight months after that. The company was in turmoil."

It was at that point that Graham, who has a degree in business and economics, stepped in as president and faced a decidedly uphill battle to keep the company from going down the tubes. Graham elected to go with the bold stroke and create a big shadow rather than try to slowly rebuild the company.

She wanted to stake Stratco's future on alkylation, which is a chemical process that creates high-octane fuels. Stratco engineers had developed this process during World War I. The problem was that much larger companies like Phillips Petroleum, UOP Inc., and Exxon's Research and Engineering Division also were experts in the chemical process, though Exxon was not a competitor until around 1990.

"We were, and still are, Davids in a field of Goliaths," says Graham, one of a only a few female executives in the petroleum business. "We've always considered ourselves an underdog. When I joined the company, I asked the employees what they knew about the competition and their marketing strategies, their prices. It turns out we knew nothing about the competition except that they were bigger.

"All we had was a good reputation as an equipment supplier, but we weren't known as an engineering company." Graham then launched a series of steps to reverse the company's fortunes, including:

■ **The alkylation seminar.** "We had some strong contacts in the oil industry so we began to develop an agenda. We thought we'd be lucky to get 20 to 30 people from the refineries and oil companies to attend."

When the big oil companies sent representatives, Graham realized that little Stratco would have to put on the performance of a lifetime at the seminar. Graham and her tiny band of engineers pulled it off without a hitch. They recruited some of the leading experts in the petroleum field to speak at the seminar.

Stratco's impressive orchestration of the seminar convinced the attendees that it could competently advise oil companies on the alkylation process. But how could such a small company make good on such a tall order? Graham explains that because so many petroleum and chemical engineers were out of work in the early 1980's, there was a large pool of them available to do consulting work on a contract basis under the Stratco banner.

"Our challenge ever since the seminar hasn't been so much the larger competitors but organizing ourselves internally to handle all the new business. We weren't overpromising at the seminar, because we knew we could find the right people. There were thousands of laid-off engineers eager for work like this," says Graham.

Another positive by-product of the seminar was an increase in orders for its equipment. "That's one of the advantages of talking directly to your target industries."

■ **Advertising and special events.** Stratco keeps people in the oil business talking about them through advertising in industry trade journals and exhibiting at leading industry gatherings like the National Petroleum Refiners Association.

To reinforce its image as a woman-owned company, Stratco each year sponsors a golf tournament in Kansas City called "Women Helping Women®." Stratco is considering sponsoring the tournament in other cities, according to Graham. In 1995, Stratco hosted a golf clinic in conjunction with a Ladies Professional Golf Association event in Phoenix.

Stratco had a hospitality tent at the LPGA event where not only its own literature was available, but literature and products from other women-owned companies, as well as from some of the oil companies. "I like to make things fun for the customers and they enjoy it when we help promote their products. Oil companies get a lot of criticism, but they don't get much credit for what they do. Every American buys products from the oil industry."

"Cause marketing" has also given Stratco's image a boost thanks to donations to area food pantries and battered women's shelters. "We believe it's important to show that's it's not just the big companies that can make a difference in their communities, but the small ones, as well," she says.

■ **Referral marketing.** Stratco sometimes gets its foot in the door of a big company by doing a small research and development project. "We often start with smaller projects. We can get them because there aren't many big engineering companies that want to take on something that small.

"We work hard and gain the confidence of a client company. Once we prove ourselves on a small project, we move up to bigger ones in the company." Stratco does not jeopardize the relationship it cultivates with a client company "by going in and trying to push a lot of equipment on them. Our engineers try to make recommendations so that the client company will have the least amount of capital expenditures. We trouble-shoot and we try to help a company re-engineer their process."

With strong references in hand from oil industry clients, Stratco has diversified into other industries by providing process engineering consulting services to the pharmaceutical, food and cosmetics industries.

Now that Stratco and its 50 employees have established its engineering expertise, the company will focus in the years ahead on becoming more sales-driven rather than engineering-driven. "We will become much more aggressive on selling," she vows.

■ **Making the most of its smallness.** Unlike its bigger competitors, Stratco can move faster on a project, from the bidding process to completion, by virtue of its size. "And we normally do it for less cost," she says. Although small, Stratco puts together very detailed engineering packages, she adds.

Stratco's alkylation technologies have been licensed in more than 30 countries, including China, France, Italy, Japan, Kuwait and Russia.

■ **Personal visibility.** Graham casts a large shadow on the oil industry by taking on leadership roles within the leading trade organizations. In 1986, she was the first woman elected to the National Lubricating Grease Institute Board of Directors and was elected president of the organization in 1992.

Her success in the petroleum industry won her an invitation to join the prestigious "Committee of 200," a national organization of more than 200 leading women entrepreneurs and business owners. "I believe you should be as visible as possible and passionate about what you are doing. The market will pick up on that very quickly," she adds.

■ **Marketing as a woman-owned company.** Stratco keeps a list of companies that are committed to giving preference on some contracts to minority- or woman-owned businesses. "We make ourselves known to those companies who keep close track of their purchasing from companies like ourselves. We try to take advantage of those opportunities." Many companies are eager to buy from a minority- or woman-owned company, but they don't know they are out there. Speak up, advises Graham.

A graduate of the Harvard Business School Owner/President Management Program, Graham says one of the most valuable marketing lessons she learned was to "walk the mall. In other words, don't sit in your office or store, but get out there and see what everyone else is doing. See what your competitors are up to. I try to 'walk the mall' every day, because it always leads to a new idea."

7 Conclusion:

Tactical Advice for Underdog Marketers

Here are 20 practical, tactical tips for outmarketing the leader:

1. **Don't just listen to the customers, act on what they are telling you.** 1-800-FLOWERS' in-house market research group does nothing but hear out its customers. President Jim McCann says before the company launches a product it asks customers such questions as: 'What would make the product more attractive to you?;' 'What price points do you find attractive?;' or 'How can we make it more convenient for you?'

   Listening is highly valued at 1-800-FLOWERS where an employee's compensation is to tied how well they score against an index measuring that skill.

2. **Deal with customers on a first-name basis.** Intimacy is a tough task for the big dogs whose customer bases are enormous. Canada's Home Hardware dealers encourage customer loyalty by learning the names and personal tastes of their regular customers. The bond-building begins when the customer

walks through the front door. "If a dealer makes one percent more a year by calling out the customer's name, then we think it's well worth the effort," says Home's Al Nash.

3. **Segment the target audience.** Houston's Second Baptist does not believe religion should be one-size-fits-all. The high-spirited church has broken its 22,000-member congregation into hundreds of niches and has customized programs for each group. Among other programs, the church has nearly 40 support groups for such problems as drug or alcohol dependence, overeating, divorce, or death of a spouse.

4. **Show the customer a good time.** Second Baptist sells the sizzle before selling the steak by creating a "froth" of special events to attract the "unchurched." Thrifty Rental Car has enthusiasm days where employees and customers might share a round of miniature golf on a makeshift course in a rental center. Computer City eliminates all the hard-sell tactics, so the customer can enjoy a more pleasant experience.

5. **Create a database of customers and use it as a promotional springboard.** The Tattered Cover knows the names and buying habits of all 110,000 of its customers thanks to its proprietary database. With that kind of electronically-generated insight, the bookstore can outmarket the bookstore chains by tailoring its promotional efforts to an individual reader's tastes. The Tattered Cover produces a series of newsletters for each of its audiences.

Viking Office Products orchestrates its computerized database of 1.5 million customers by personalizing the catalogs to meet an individual's buying pattern. Chief executive Irwin Helford lends his smiling face to each of the company's 73 different catalogs. "Our proprietary database marketing programs help us to understand and 'talk' to one customer at a time while marketing to millions." Viking has mastered the art of micromarketing.

6. **Create a distinctive image.** Because Gateway 2000 considers its Midwestern roots and values a selling point, it selected a cow spot to help brand its personality. It's bucolic, but certainly memorable. As Gateway's Al Giazzon points out: "We have a simple, recognizable personality and that's a powerful position to have in the market. I believe it's harder for people to come up with a quick sentence about Dell than it is about Gateway."

   Allen-Edmonds reinforces its image of scrupulous craftsmanship through meticulously crafted brochures, newsletter and print ads. All of it has a rich, understated look to it, which helps contribute to the mystique of the Allen-Edmonds shoe. "Our brochures and booklets go into great detail about the steps we take to produce a quality shoe," says Allen-Edmond's John Stollenwerk.

7. **Use non-traditional media channels.** When the new owners of Christian Supply Centers launched an advertising campaign to announce its new look and line of merchandise, it cast its bread upon the waters primarily through radio. The spots were heard not just on Christian radio stations in Portland, but on talk, all-news and country-and-western radio formats. General audiences, not used to hearing ads for Christian book stores, responded by visiting the stores, which had begun carrying new lines of merchandise of interest to both religious and non-religious people.

8. **Strut your stuff by sponsoring an industry seminar.** Chemical engineering firm Stratco Incorporated put itself on the map with engineers and executives of the leading petroleum companies by orchestrating a seminar on a chemical engineering process in which it had expertise. The seminar produced a gusher of new business.

9. **Keep tabs on the competition.** Children's Discovery Center's Lois Mitten checks out her publicly-owned rivals' filings with the Securities Exchange Commission. SEC documents have

given Mitten a stronger sense of the demographic profile of customers they're seeking and types of locations that interest KinderCare and other publicly operated childcare rivals.

10. **Keep tabs on yourself.** Once a year, CDC's Mitten hires a mystery shopper to scope out the competition. The mystery shopper also drops in on the five CDC's to provide Mitten an unbiased look at her own operation.

   Computer City also hires mystery shoppers to prowl its stores once a quarter. The mystery shoppers help determine how effectively the stores' sales associates are jumping through hoops for customers.

11. **Raid the top dog's best customers.** This tactic is for the bold at heart, which describes Virgin Atlantic Airways. It sent direct mail to names obtained from a list broker of people who frequently fly overseas. Virgin zeroed in on those who were members of British Air's frequent flyer program by inviting them to send the original copy of their most recent statement. In exchange, Virgin awarded respondents who had logged 50,000 miles or more on British Airways with 50,000 frequent flyer miles on Virgin. It's no wonder British Air doesn't like Virgin.

12. **Launch pre-emptive strikes.** Here's another page from Virgin's playbook. When it learned that the major carriers were meeting with video recorder manufacturers to create seatback screens on airlines, Virgin beat the big dogs to the punch. It handed out Sony Walkmans to passengers who could then select a movie to help while away the flight.

   "We got the jump on our competitors by several years," says Virgin's David Tait. "In a sense we lead the industry from the rear. That's the beauty of being small. You can react very quickly. It's easier to wield David's slingshot than Goliath's heavy metal sword."

13. **Why pay retail?** Gateway 2000 doesn't believe in it, because it doesn't want to surrender 4 to 10 percent of its profits to retail-

ers to sell its computers. Gateway sells its computers through the direct channel—the one and only avenue it uses to reach consumers.

14. **Use promotional pricing, but only to attract new customers.** Viking Office Products figures that once a new customer gets a taste of its fanatical customer service, he or she will be willing to pay a higher price for items in its catalogs on a long-term basis. Viking also uses what it calls "variable pricing," in which Viking will often sell the same product at different prices in different markets at the same time.

15. **Put everyone in the organization on the same page.** Meridian Bank "warehouses" information from various application systems in a central database, which allows employees and customers better access to the bank's offerings. The information is available in every branch and on the laptop computers of the bank's commercial loan officers, who spend more time in the field at customer's offices than they do in their offices.

16. **Offer proof that your service or product works.** Talk is cheap, but it becomes more substantial when an underdog marketer can validate its claims. Devon Direct proved its worth to MCI by running a limited direct mail test. Impressed with the results, MCI ordered a full rollout of a direct mail campaign that dispatched 150 million pieces in two years. Devon Direct is now one of the nation's leading direct-response powerhouses.

17. **Tell the world who your clients are.** After landing a client, particularly a blue-chip company, Devon Direct's Ron Greene says underdogs should let prospective clients know who's in their stable. It won't scare off potential clients who might think the firm is too busy for them; rather, it builds credibility for a growing business.

18. **Benchmark and reverse-engineer.** This is unconventional advice for underdogs—a particularly innovative breed—but

it's worked for a discounter like Drypers, which can't afford the research-and-development overhead when locked in a brutal price war. Drypers' Dave Pitassi says they're content to watch the big dogs go through the learning curve of developing a prototype. "But we'll get to the market just as quickly. By the time we start spending to develop and market the product, we're already a step ahead of them."

19. **Focus on the internal.** Too many organizations try to change themselves to meet external demands, presenting a disjointed face to the world and an undefined corporate culture to their employees. As many of the foregoing examples, including MCI, Home Hardware, the Tattered Cover, and K&A, have shown, success in marketing comes when everyone in the company knows the needs and goals of the company they work for— when every member of the staff is a salesperson for the company. As Thomas D. Kuczmarski of K&A says, "build a culture where people feel good about working here and more importantly, good about themselves."

20. **Don't take no for an answer.** This is the most sacred of sales tenets but underdog marketers should also impress this one into their memory. "Working Mom on the Run" Debbie Nigro, a once-struggling radio talk show host, says the word 'no' is often just an invitation to try another tack. "We heard a lot of 'no's' in trying to sell this program. Most of them later became 'yes's'."

Hats off to the indomitable spirit of the underdog marketer!

ABOUT THE AUTHOR

Edmund Lawler speaks, consults, teaches and writes on the subjects of marketing and communications. He is co-author of *Marketing Masters: Secrets of America's Best Companies,* which has been translated into five languages.

Since 1990, Mr. Lawler has been captain of Copy Chasers, a panel of advertising experts convened by *Advertising Age*'s *Business Marketing* magazine. Mr. Lawler is a former managing editor of *Business Marketing,* and he writes an advertising critique column for the magazine. A compilation of his columns was published under the title, *Copy Chasers on Creating Business-to-Business Ads.*

Mr. Lawler has been a correspondent for the Chicago bureau of the Associated Press, and currently is an adjunct faculty member in the Communication Department at DePaul University.

He is a graduate of Drake University and the University of Notre Dame. He lives in Chicago with his wife, Priscilla, and their two sons, Griffin and Bryan.

To order additional copies of *Underdog Marketing: Successful Strategies for Outmarketing the Leader,* send a check for $19.95 for each book ordered plus $2 postage and handling for the first book, and $1 for each additional copy to:
MasterMedia Limited
17 East 89th Street
New York, NY 10128
(212) 546-7650
(800) 334-8232 *please use MasterCard or VISA on phone orders*
(212) 546-7638 (fax)

Edmund Lawler is available for speaking engagements. Please see next page for complete information.

Underdog Marketing: Strategies for Outmarketing the Leader

Marketing against leaders such as AT&T, Procter & Gamble, and British Airways may seem like an unenviable task. Yet, underdog marketers like MCI, Drypers, and Virgin Atlantic Airways relish the challenge of taking on the best.

The author of *Underdog Marketing: Successful Strategies for Outmarketing the Leader* reveals secrets of these and other feisty competitors, including:

■ How to practice "corporate jujitsu"

■ How to differentiate your product or service from the leader's

■ How to cast a larger-than-life shadow on the market

PROGRAM LENGTH: 1 hour. Keynote.

Copy Masters

As the author of *Copy Chasers on Creating Business-to-Business Ads,* Ed Lawler has shown more than 100 companies, associations and ad agencies how to create more visually magnetic, benefit-oriented messages for customers and prospects.

In his hands-on clinic, Ed presents the good, the bad, and the truly ugly of business advertising and provides an in-depth analysis of an organization's marketing communications.

The program includes a lively, interactive exercise that tests participants' skills at evaluating ads based on the Copy Chasers Criteria. The clinic is designed to help managers make decisions about promotional investments.

PROGRAM LENGTH: 2 hours. Seminar.

For more information, call Tony Calao, director of MasterMedia's Speakers Bureau at 800-453-2887.

OTHER MASTERMEDIA BOOKS

To order additional copies of any MasterMedia book, send a check for the price of the book plus $2.00 postage and handling for the first book, $1.00 for each additional book to:

MasterMedia Limited
17 East 89th Street
New York, NY 10128
(212) 260-5600
(800) 334-8232 *please use MasterCard or VISA on 1-800 orders*
(212) 546-7638 (fax)

AGING PARENTS AND YOU: A Complete Handbook to Help You Help Your Elders Maintain a Healthy, Productive and Independent Life, by Eugenia Anderson-Ellis, is a complete guide to providing care to aging relatives. It gives practical advice and resources to adults who are helping their elders lead productive and independent lives. Revised and updated. ($9.95 paper)

BALANCING ACTS! Juggling Love, Work, Family, and Recreation, by Susan Schiffer Stautberg and Marcia L. Worthing, provides strategies to achieve a balanced life by reordering priorities and setting realistic goals. ($12.95 paper)

BOUNCING BACK: How to Turn Business Crises Into Success, by Harvey Reese. Based on interviews with entrepreneurs from coast to coast, this fascinating book contains cautionary tales that unfold with gripping suspense. Reese has discovered a formula for success that should be "must reading" for every new or budding entrepreneur. ($18.95 hardbound)

BREATHING SPACE: Living and Working at a Comfortable Pace in a Sped-Up Society, by Jeff Davidson, helps readers to handle information and activity overload and gain greater control over their lives. ($10.95 paper)

CITIES OF OPPORTUNITY: Finding the Best Place to Work, Live and Prosper in the 1990's and Beyond, by Dr. John Tepper Marlin, explores the job and living options for the next decade and into the next century. This consumer guide and handbook, written by one of the world's experts on cities, selects and features forty-six American cities and metropolitan areas. ($13.95 paper, $24.95 cloth)

THE CONFIDENCE FACTOR: How Self-Esteem Can Change Your Life, by Dr. Judith Briles, is based on a nationwide survey of six thousand men and women. Briles explores why women so often feel a lack of self-confidence and have a poor opinion of themselves. She offers step-by-step advice on becoming the person you want to be. ($9.95 paper, $18.95 cloth)

THE DOLLARS AND SENSE OF DIVORCE, by Dr. Judith Briles, is the first book to combine practical tips on overcoming the legal hurdles by planning finances before, during, and after divorce. ($10.95 paper)

THE ENVIRONMENTAL GARDENER: The Solution to Pollution for Lawns and Gardens, by Laurence Sombke, focuses on what each of us can do to protect our endangered plant life. A practical sourcebook and shopping guide. ($8.95 paper)

HERITAGE: The Making of an American Family, by Dr. Robert Pamplin, Jr., traces the phenomenal history of the Pamplin family from the Crusades to an eye-opening account of how they built one of the largest private fortunes in the United States. Heritage is an inspiring paradigm for achievement based on a strong belief in God and integrity. ($24.95, hardbound; $12.95 paperbound)

LIFETIME EMPLOYABILITY: How to Become Indispensable, by Carole Hyatt is both a guide through the mysteries of the business universe brought down to earth and a handbook to help you evaluate your attitudes, your skills, and your goals. Through expert advice and interviews of nearly 200 men and women whose lives have changed because their jobs or goals shifted, Lifetime Employability is designed to increase your staying power in today's down-sized economy. ($12.95 paper)

THE LIVING HEART BRAND NAME SHOPPER'S GUIDE, by Michael F. DeBakey, M.D., Antonio M. Gotto, Jr., M.D., D.Phil., Lynne W. Scott, M.A., R.D./L.D., and John P. Foreyt, Ph.D., lists brand-name supermarket products that are low in fat, saturated fatty acids, and cholesterol. ($12.50 paper)

THE LOYALTY FACTOR: Building Trust in Today's Workplace, by Carol Kinsey Goman, Ph.D., offers techniques for restoring commitment and loyalty in the workplace. ($9.95 paper)

MANAGING YOUR CHILD'S DIABETES, by Robert Wood Johnson IV, Sale Johnson, Casey Johnson, and Susan Kleinman, brings help to families trying to understand diabetes and control its effects. ($10.95 paper)

MANN FOR ALL SEASONS: Wit and Wisdom from The Washington Post*'s Judy Mann,* by Judy Mann, shows the columnist at her best as she writes about women, families, and the impact and politics of the women's revolution. ($9.95 paper, $19.95 cloth)

OUT THE ORGANIZATION: New Career Opportunities for the 1990's, by Robert and Madeleine Swain, is written for the millions of Americans whose jobs are no longer safe, whose companies are not loyal, and who face futures of uncertainty. it gives advice on finding a new job or starting your own business. ($12.95 paper)

POSITIVELY OUTRAGEOUS SERVICE: New and Easy Ways to Win Customers for Life, by T. Scott Gross, identifies what the consumers of the nineties really want and how businesses can develop effective marketing strategies to answer those needs. ($14.95)

THE PREGNANCY AND MOTHERHOOD DIARY: Planning the First Year of Your Second Career, by Susan Schiffer Stautberg, is the first and only undated appointment diary that shows how to manage pregnancy and career. ($12.95 spiralbound)

PRELUDE TO SURRENDER: The Pamplin Family and the Siege of Petersburg, by Dr. Robert Pamplin, Jr., offers an exciting and moving narrative, interspersed with facts, of the American Civil War and the ten-month siege and battles of Petersburg, Virginia, as seen through the eyes of Dr. Pamplin's ancestors, the Boisseau family. ($10.95 hardbound)

REAL LIFE 101: The Graduate's Guide to Survival, by Susan Kleinman, supplies welcome advice to those facing "real life" for the first time, focusing on work, money, health, and how to deal with freedom and responsibility. ($9.95 paper)

SIDE-BY-SIDE STRATEGIES: How Two-Career Couples Can Thrive in the Nineties, by Jane Hershey Cuozzo and S. Diane Graham, describes how two-career couples can learn the difference between competing with a spouse and becoming a supportive power partner. Published in hardcover as Power Partners. ($10.95 paper, $19.95 cloth)

STEP FORWARD: Sexual Harassment in the Workplace, What You Need to Know, by Susan L. Webb, presents the facts for identifying the tell-tale signs of sexual harassment on the job, and how to deal with it. ($9.95 paper)

TAKING CONTROL OF YOUR LIFE: The Secrets of Successful Enterprising Women, by Gail Blanke and Kathleen Walas, is based on the authors' professional experience with Avon Products' Women of Enterprise Awards, given each year to outstanding women entrepreneurs. The authors offer a specific plan to help women gain control over their lives, and include business tips and quizzes as well as beauty and lifestyle information. ($17.95 cloth)

TWENTYSOMETHING: Managing and Motivating Today's New Work Force, by Lawrence J. Bradford, Ph.D., and Claire Raines, M.A., examines the work orientation of the younger generation, offering managers in businesses of all kinds a practical guide to better understand and supervise their young employees. ($22.95 cloth)

YOUR HEALTHY BODY, YOUR HEALTHY LIFE: How to Take Control of Your Medical Destiny, by Donald B. Louria, M.D., provides precise advice and strategies that will help you to live a long and healthy life. Learn also about nutrition, exercise, vitamins, and medication, as well as how to control risk factors for major diseases. Revised and updated. ($12.95 paper)